Building Gender Fairness in Schools

by

Beverly A. Stitt
Southern Illinois University

with

Thomas L. Erekson
University of Illinois

Richard K. Hofstrand
Eastern Illinois University

Franzie L. Loepp
Illinois State University

Carole W. Minor
Northern Illinois University

Heidi R. Perreault
Southern Illinois University

John G. Savage
Western Illinois University

Southern Illinois University Press

Carbondale and Edwardsville

Printed in the United States Of America
Edited by Kathryn Koldehoff

Library of Congress Cataloging-in-Publication Data

Stitt, Beverly A. , 1943-
Building gender fairness in schools.

Bibliograph: p.
1. Sex discrimination in education--United States.
2. Sexism--United States. I. Erekson, Thomas L.
II. Title.
LC212.82.S75 1988 370.19'345 88-2003
ISBN 0-8093-1474-6

92 91 90 89 5 4 3 2

Contents

Tables

Foreword

Illinois educators are committed to the intent of the Carl D. Perkins Vocational Education Act of 1984 which includes substantial emphasis on promoting access to programs for young people and adults, particularly those who have special barriers to employment because of their sex. The Illinois State Board of Education is aggressively addressing sex-equity issues, and this publication is an example of that commitment.

This book will help educators, those preparing to be teachers and those already teaching, identify and eliminate gender bias from their classrooms. It will help educators assess their own level of gender bias, determine the effects of gender bias on students and society, and provide activities for eliminating these gender biases. The goal is to help students be all they can be without the constraints of "acceptable" behavior and roles based on gender.

Numerous studies have shown that sex bias is prevalent in curriculum materials, classroom interactions, and in the classroom environment. Educators need to be aware of their own gender bias and determine strategies for eliminating that bias from the classroom. In addition, educators can provide students with the opportunities to explore their interests without the constraints of traditional sex-role options. Too many careers continue to be stereotyped as male or female.

The materials in the units of this book were developed by six contributing authors from teacher-education institutions in Illinois. The units were field-tested with pre-service and in-service teachers at Southern Illinois University at Carbondale.

This work truly represents the commitment in Illinois to gender-fair teaching and equal opportunity for female and male students in occupational and career choices.

Ted Sanders
State Superintendent of Education
Illinois State Board of Education

Preface

Myra and David Sadker, Professors of Education at the American University in Washington, D.C., conducted a study of the twenty-four most widely used teacher-education textbooks and found that twenty-three give less than 1 percent of their space to the issue of sexism; one-third do not mention the issue of sexism at all (most of the texts guilty of this oversight are in math and science--the areas in which girls are most likely to have achievement difficulties); and not a single text provides future teachers with curricular resources and instructional strategies to counteract sexism in the classroom and its harmful impact on students (1).

This study by the Sadkers echoes the findings of other research in teacher education. Three additional important findings are (1) that after entering school, the key element reinforcing sex-role stereotyping is the way school personnel interact with students; (2) that teachers can be trained to eliminate gender-biased behaviors; and (3) that bias-free teaching is good for all students--teachers who do not exhibit sex-role stereotyping in their classrooms are better teachers. This book is a response to these omissions and identified needs in teacher education textbooks.

Teacher-education faculty from six universities in Illinois are contributing authors of this book. They were invited because of their commitment to good teaching, their awareness of the importance of gender fairness, and their

Reference

1. Sadker, M. and Sadker, D. Beyond Pictures and Pronouns: Sexism in Teacher Education Textbooks. Washington, D.C., Department of Education, Women's Educational Equity Act Program, 1980.

outstanding professional reputations in the state. The book was developed by the Illinois Building Fairness Resource Center, directed by Dr. Beverly A. Stitt, and was supported through the Illinois State Board of Education, Department of Adult, Vocational and Technical Education with funds originating from the Carl D. Perkins Vocational Education Act of 1984.

Appreciation is gratefully acknowledged to Longman, Inc., for permission to adopt in the Readings section parts of the out-of-print <u>Sex Equity Handbook for Schools</u>. Special recognition goes to Jan Lathrop, Illinois Competency-Based Education Consultant, who assisted the authors with the outcome-based format of the units, to Sylvia Gist, who made valuable recommendations in the development stages; and to Sandra Wankel who tirelessly entered continual revisions to the manuscript.

How to Use This Book

"A man and his son were riding a motorcycle and got into a serious accident. They were both unconscious and rushed to the hospital. It was established that the son needed surgery immediately. He was wheeled into the operating room when the surgeon walked in and said 'I cannot operate on this patient for he is my son.' How is this possible?"(1).*

When presented with this riddle, four students out of nine in an all-women cell-biology class figured out the answer. In an all-women general-biology class, the numbers were five out of fifteen. When presented at the end of the semester in a coed sex and gender class, only three out of seventeen students came up with the solution.

A similar exercise in which the father is in a nontraditional role would probably result in a similar response. People are often treated not on the basis of their individual characteristics but according to stereotypes about appropriate roles and behaviors. This environment is especially discouraging to students who are trying to pursue interests and develop abilities that do not coincide with current cultural expectations.

Most people do not think that women and men are treated much differently today, especially in schools. Certainly, most teachers, counselors, and principals do not want to be guilty of sex or race discrimination or of discrimination

---

*Numbers in parentheses at the end of a sentence are keyed to the alphabetically arranged references that follow some sections.

based on a person's physical or emotional handicaps. They want to treat students individually.

But regardless of the best of intentions and well-stated philosophies of education, behaviors are based on deep-rooted assumptions that differentiate between the appropriate behaviors, roles, and jobs for women and men. These assumptions may not even be conscious, but they result in subtle differences in the way we treat people--what we expect from them, how we think they should act, what we think they should look like, and how we think they should respond to us.

The results of these unintentional differences in treatment have serious short-term and long-term consequences for all students. It is the purpose of this book to provide a means for pre-service and in-service teachers to become aware of unconscious behaviors that are harmful to male and female students, to choose to be gender-fair teachers and to develop competencies in teaching strategies that result in gender fairness in schools.

The book is divided into two sections--readings and eleven units of instruction. Each unit presents a competency to be mastered by the pre-service or in-service teacher. Although the units are presented in a logical sequence, the book is written so that instructors may select particular competencies to use as part of an existing course or for independent-study courses. The book can, of course, be used as the text for a complete course in gender-fair teaching.

Each unit has a specific competency to be mastered identified in the title, with a stated performance objective. If there are prerequisites, those items are listed before the learning activities for the unit. The learning activities are presented to accommodate the four-step teaching format of preparation, presentation, practice, and evaluation. The activities are sequenced according to Bloom's taxonomy of education from knowledge and comprehension, through application and analysis to synthesis and evaluation. It is not, however, necessary to complete all of the activities in each unit. Some of the learning activities refer students to specific readings in the first section of this book; other activities consist of worksheets and classroom or out-of-class activities to complete. The instructor may wish to select specific learning activities or develop others as determined by class needs. The learning activities are suggestions rather than requirements.

After the list of learning activities, the evaluation method to determine competence is stated. Evaluation strategies include writing, discussion participation, role playing, practice teaching, developing calendars, planning strategies, and developing action plans. These evaluations were developed to encourage measurable skill development in the competencies rather than simply to test knowledge using traditional paper-and-pencil questions. It is recommended that the instructor use the evaluation suggested or select another evaluation method that provides assurance that the student is indeed competent in the strategy.

Unit One, Develop an Awareness of the Effects of Gender Bias, and Unit Two, Identify Personal Gender Biases, provide the students with an introduction to the whole problem of gender bias in schools and what personal effects this bias can have or may have had on them. Students with prior knowledge or experience in this area may be able to review the prerequisite readings and go on to later units. Using the units as written, it will take approximately two class periods to complete Unit One and two or three class periods to complete Unit Two.

Unit Three, Use Gender-Fair Verbal Interaction With Students, and Unit Four, Use Gender-Fair Nonverbal Interaction With Students, can be used together to provide brief but focused training for eliminating gender bias in classroom interactions through actual practice of gender-fair interactions. Three or four class periods are required to complete Unit Three and three class periods are required to complete Unit Four.

Unit Five, Identify Gender-Fair Curriculum Materials, provides the means to recognize gender-fair materials and also to develop techniques for diffusing the power of gender-biased materials until they can be replaced. Two class periods are required to complete Unit Five.

Unit Six, Encourage Students to Broaden Their Occupational Choices, outlines methods of keeping up-to-date on occupational trends and of evaluating occupational descriptions and activities for gender bias. Two class periods are required to complete the learning activities in Unit Six.

Unit Seven, Plan Activities to Recruit and Retain Nontraditional Students, develops awareness of who should recruit students for particular programs as well as awareness of various recruitment ideas that are free of gender bias. The opportunity to develop recruitment strategies is also offered, requiring one or two class periods for completion.

Unit Eight, Develop Strategies to Achieve Schoolwide Support for Gender Fairness, Unit Nine, Identify and Develop Strategies to Counteract Societal Influences and Cultural Myths that Hamper Students, and Unit Ten, Develop Action Plans to Effect Societal Change Outside the Classroom offer students the opportunity to develop specific strategies for use in school and out of school to become advocates of a gender-fair society. Interviews of school personnel, analysis of several media systems, and the development of a personal action plan to effect improvement are included. Three class periods are required for completing Unit Eight; one or two class periods are required for Unit Nine; and two class periods are required to complete Unit Ten.

Unit Eleven, Conduct Applied Research to Develop Policies and Programs to Achieve Gender Fairness, takes the advanced education student through the steps of conducting a research study and developing the results into a publishable article to continue the move toward gender fairness in policies and programs nationwide. Two class periods are required to complete Unit Eleven. The summary includes a rating sheet for gender-fair teaching which includes aspects of the competency units.

Unit Three, Use Gender-Fair Verbal Interaction with Students, was field-tested with 68 in-service vocational faculty at a Technology Update Institute in June 1987. The participants were given the script on p. 148 and were asked to count the number of gender-biased interactions they could find. Then they were given a twenty-five-minute presentation of some of the reading material and activities found in Unit Three. After the instruction, participants were asked to see how many more examples of gender-bias they could find in the script. As the following table indicates, these teachers were able to recognize a greater number of gender-biased verbal interactions with instruction.

Participant	Mean Response Pre-Test	Post-Test	Improvement
Male (n=28)	2.930	6.630	2.700
Female (n=40)	3.675	6.825	3.150
Overall (n=68)	3.779	6.750	2.971

Comments made by the teachers after the brief pilot test included:

"Fascinating! I had no idea such statements were so obviously gender biased."

"I say these things--I am so shocked--I would never purposely display bias."

"Where can I get more information on this?"

"Surely, this cannot be truly happening all over the nation, yet I just know it is."

Teacher educators using this book please forward any test or survey data that you generate in completing these units. This information will be shared with other teacher educators who want to know if these units will result in gender-fair teaching.

In summary, research indicates that bias in classroom interaction inhibits student achievement. Research also indicates that training to eliminate gender bias results in overall better teaching; equity in teaching promotes excellence as well. The tools to solve the problems of gender bias in schools have been forged. It is up to educators to pick them up and put them to use. Of greatest importance, it is up to teacher educators to see that their pre-service students have these tools and know how to use them. It is with this purpose in mind that this book is offered to teacher-education institutions.

Reference

1. Halpern, C. and Samuelson, M. Our Progress and Struggles as Feminists Teaching Biology. Feminist Teacher 1(4):34 1985.

Part 1

Readings

Gender Bias in Schools

Gender bias is a set of beliefs or attitudes that indicates a primary view or set of expectations of peoples' abilities and interests according to their sex. This first reading is a report card. You will not find it in any elementary- or secondary-school classrooms. Nevertheless, it is an important evaluation. It reflects the loss that girls and boys suffer because of gender bias in society and in our schools.

Girls: Academic

Girls start out ahead of boys in speaking, reading, and counting. In the early grades, their academic performance is equal to boys' in math and science. However, as they progress through school, their achievement-test scores show significant decline. The scores of boys, on the other hand, continue to rise and eventually reach and surpass those of their female counterparts, particularly in the areas of math and science (30).

In spite of performance decline on standardized achievement tests, girls frequently receive better grades in school. This may be one of the rewards for being more quiet and docile in the classroom. However, this may be at the cost of independence and self-reliance (30).

Girls are more likely to be invisible members of classrooms. They receive fewer academic contacts, less praise, fewer complex and abstract questions, and less instruction on how to do things for themselves (7, 15, 28, 37, 45).

Girls who are gifted in mathematics are far less likely to be identified than are gifted boys. Those girls who are identified as gifted, are far less likely to participate in special or accelerated math classes to develop this special talent (17).

Girls who suffer from learning disabilities are also less likely to be identified or to participate in special education programs than are learning-disabled boys (6, 9, 29).

Boys: Academic

Boys are more likely to be scolded and reprimanded in classrooms, even when the observed conduct and behavior of boys and girls does not differ. Also, boys are more likely to be referred to school authorities for disciplinary action than are girls (10, 13, 22).

Boys are far more likely to be identified as exhibiting learning disabilities, reading problems, and mental retardation (9, 19, 30, 32).

Not only are boys more frequently identified as having learning and reading disabilities; they also receive lower grades, are more likely to be grade repeaters, and are less likely to complete high school (5).

Girls: Psychological and Physical

Although women achieve better grades than men, they are less likely to believe that they can do college work. In fact, of the brightest high school graduates who do not go on to college, 70 to 90 percent are women (44).

Learned helplessness exists when failure is perceived as insurmountable. Girls are more likely than boys to exhibit this pattern. They attribute failure to internal factors, such as ability, rather than to external factors, such as luck or effort. Girls who exhibit learned helplessness avoid failure situations--they stop trying. Research indicates that teacher interaction patterns may contribute to the learned helplessness exhibited by female students (11, 12, 33).

In athletics, females also suffer from sex bias. For example, women's athletic budgets in the nation's colleges are equal to approximately 18 percent of the men's budgets (1).

Boys: Psychological and Physical

Society socializes boys into active, independent, and aggressive roles. But these behaviors are incongruent with school norms and rituals that stress quiet behavior and docility. This results in a pattern of role conflict for boys, particularly during the elementary years (18, 21).

Boys are taught stereotyped behaviors earlier and more harshly than girls; there is a 20 percent greater probability that such stereotyped behavior will stay with them for life (16, 24).

Conforming to the male sex-role stereotype takes a psychological toll. Boys with high scores on sex-appropriate behavior tests also score highest on anxiety tests (2, 3, 43).

The strain and anxiety associated with conforming to the male sex stereotype also affects boys physically. Males are more likely to succumb to serious disease and to be victims of accidents or violence. The average life expectancy of men is eight years shorter than that of women (43).

Girls: Careers and Family Relationships

The majority of girls enter college without completing four years of high school mathematics. This lack of preparation in math serves as a "critical filter," inhibiting or preventing girls from entering many science-, math-, and technology-related careers (36).

The preparation and counseling girls receive in school contribute to the economic penalities they encounter in the workplace. Although over 90 percent of the girls in our classrooms will work in the paid labor force for all or part of their lives, statistics reveal that there are costs in the bias they encounter (40).

Greater than one-third of female-headed families live below the poverty level.

A woman with a college degree will typically earn less than a male who is a high school dropout.

The typical working woman will earn fifty-nine cents for every dollar earned by a male worker. Minority women earn even less, averaging only 50 percent of the wages earned by white males.

Women represent 79 percent of all clerical workers, but only 5 percent of all craft workers.

Women must work nine days to earn what men are paid for five days' work.

In contrast to the popular belief that things are getting better for female workers, since 1954 the gap between the wages earned by men and women has not lessened.

The majority of women work not for "extra" cash, but because of economic necessity. Nearly two-thirds of all women in the labor force are single, widowed, divorced, or separated, or they are married to spouses earning less than ten thousand dollars a year.

Boys: Careers and Family Relationships

Many boys build career expectations that are higher than their abilities. This later results in compromise, disappointment, and frustration (35).

Both at school and at home, boys are taught to hide or suppress their emotions; as men they may find it difficult or impossible to show feelings toward their family and friends (20, 25, 26).

Boys are actively discouraged from playing with dolls (except those that play sports or wage war). Few schools provide programs that encourage boys to learn about the skills of parenting. Many men, through absence and apathy, become not so much parents as "transparents." In fact, the typical father spends only twelve minutes a day interacting with his children (39).

Men and women differ in their beliefs of the important aspects of a father's role. Men emphasize the need for the father to earn a good income and to provide solutions to family problems. Women, on the other hand, stress the need for fathers to assist in caring for children and responding to the emotional needs of the family. These differing perceptions of fatherhood lead to family strain and anxiety (14).

The Changes

As grim as the statistics and research findings are, they are not etched in stone. There will be other report cards, other opportunities to create an educational system that is more equitable in its treatment of both girls and boys. Change is not only possible, it is already taking place.

Formerly studies indicated that as children progressed through school, their opinion of boys became higher and their opinion of girls became lower. Recent research indicates that girls now ascribe a more positive value to their own sex. This more positive self-image may reflect society's greater sensitivity to sexism and a more positive perception of the role of women (27, 34, 38).

One-third of the women participating in a recent survey indicated a preference for a nontraditional, androgynous parenting role (14).

In the report card, we reported that women's athletic budgets in 1978-1979 were only 18 percent of men's budgets. But seen in perspective, a positive trend is apparent. In 1974, this figure was only 2 percent. Moreover, the number of females participating in athletics increased 570 percent between 1970 and 1980 (1, 40).

In 1958, the labor force participation rate of women stood at 33 percent; by 1980 it had reached 50 percent. Although most women are still overrepresented in low-paying jobs, barriers are falling as some women are entering high-level positions previously held only by men (40).

More current U.S. Department of Labor Statistics indicate that the typical working woman earns sixty-four cents for every dollar earned by a male worker; minority women average only 53 percent of the wages earned by white males; women are 80 percent of all clerical workers, but only 8 percent of all craft workers; and women must work eight days to earn what men get paid for five days of work (41).

These findings are encouraging, but many barriers still exist. For example, as far back as 1946 (8), studies documented the extensive bias in textbooks. Women were frequently omitted, and when included, were portrayed in stereotypic roles. In response to these studies and to the voices of criticism, the publishing companies issued guidelines designed to help authors and editors avoid sexist portrayals. But a recent analysis of school textbooks has disclosed that the number of male-centered stories has increased rather than decreased. Minority females remain almost nonexistent. Language is not as blatantly masculine, fewer women are pictured wearing aprons; but schoolbooks are still telling stories in which few women find a place (4).

Change seldom comes quickly or easily. Identifying the problem is only the first step. In many ways, it is the easiest step to take. The challenges and opportunities belong to teachers.

Nonsexist Teaching

Many teachers and parents often comment that they are teaching and raising their children in a nonsexist fashion; they go out of their way to bring nonsexist books and toys into their classrooms and their homes; they try to expose children to nonstereotyped role models in the community; they assure their children that they are free to choose how they want to behave and what they want to become.

But if you listen carefully, you will also hear these committed teachers and parents express confusion and bewilderment. Despite these efforts, their daughters and their sons often seem to be trapped inside stereotypes. One feminist educator tells of having come home from a conference on nonsexist teaching to find her nine-year-old daughter insisting she cannot become a doctor because only boys can be doctors. A mother tells about driving to the other end of her city to take her daughter to a female pediatrician--and the child's unwavering claim that girls are nurses and boys are doctors. And a physician describes having been utterly dumbfounded when her six-year-old son patiently explained to her that women cannot be doctors. A junior high school teacher describes how she made elaborate preparations to expose her class to nonsexist career models in the medical profession. She took her seventh graders on a field trip to a local hospital. A male nurse talked to the children about what his job was like. A female doctor talked to the children about her job and she conducted a tour around the hospital. When the students returned to their classroom, the teacher was surprised when some of the children still insisted that men are supposed to be doctors and women are supposed to be nurses. "How can you say that?" the teacher asked. "Today you saw a male nurse, and the woman who took you around the hospital was a doctor." The children were undaunted by reality. "Oh, those people lied," was the quick response.

These may be extreme examples--but they are also illustrations of how difficult nonsexist teaching and child rearing is. Children are exposed to a continual bombardment of sexist messages in almost every aspect of their lives. They go to the toy store and see science kits with pictures of boys looking through microscopes and documenting experiments. They see rows of well-endowed female dolls with pretty dresses and wavy hair. They turn on their television sets on Saturday morning and watch the superheroes--all male except for Wonderwoman--perform amazing feats. They watch detectives and police officers and doctors--almost always male--rescue victims in trouble--almost always female. Every day, several times a day, they are bombarded with short and cleverly devised commercials in which women fight ring-around-the-collar and greasy-wax-build-up so that their homes will be spotless when their husbands return from work. In fact, television's ring-around-the-collar may be the universal electronic curriculum, the ring that binds and unites all children in a common sexist environment. Exposing children to an occasional nonsexist book or taking them to visit a female doctor is not enough. More powerful medicine is needed to counteract the sexist messages that society delivers.

There are several lessons to be learned from those teachers who have pioneered experiments in creating nonsexist classrooms. Their early attempts provide important direction on how to create nonsexist classrooms so that we can go about changing the facts and figures reported earlier.

Guidelines for Gender Fair Teaching

1. Gender-Fair Teaching Should Be Continuous and Integral to Daily Instruction

Most research shows that the attitudes and behaviors of children, particularly girls, can become less stereotyped after they read nonsexist materials. The problem is that these changes often do not last from year to year--or even month to month or week to week. This means that to truly open up options for children, teachers need to incorporate nonsexist materials, books, activities, and lessons on a continual basis in the day-to-day teaching of children. When a text presents a separate chapter or boxed-off section on issues related to sex equity, children learn that this information is isolated from and not integral to the main body of information the text presents. Similarly, if there is a separate lesson or even a separate unit on changing roles for women and men, the message is that the topic is an interesting diversion but not really an important issue for children to learn.

2. Gender-Fair Teaching Must Direct Attention to the Stereotypes and Problems that Affect Boys as Well as Girls

Those who have worked with nonsexist curriculum in elementary and secondary schools frequently comment that boys seem to be more resistant than girls to these materials. For example, in one research project nonsexist curriculum was taught at the kindergarten, fifth-, and ninth-grade levels. Female students in these different grades showed reduced stereotyped attitudes toward occupational, social, and emotional roles after instruction in the nonsexist curriculum. However, male students were more resistant to changing stereotyped attitudes and, at the ninth-grade level, they actually exhibited stronger sex-role stereotyping after the nonsexist curricular intervention (23).

A high school teacher who taught a unit about outstanding women in U.S. history notes that the boys in her class were actually hostile to the unit. Several claimed that they were being brainwashed with reverse sexism and that they were being left out. These early teaching attempts illustrate very clearly that when we talk about gender-fair teaching we need to pay attention to the harmful impact of stereotyping on male as well as female students.

3. Gender-Fair Teaching Must Also Be Concerned with Discrimination on the Basis of Race, Ethnicity, Religion, Class, Age, and Handicap

Discrimination on the basis of sex grows from the same kind of prejudice that harms people who are members of various minority groups. Gender-fair teaching must be broad in its application and should work toward confronting prejudice and discrimination in its widest sense.

For example, when you develop gender-fair lesson plans and learning centers, it is important to include the experiences and achievements of women and men from various racial and ethnic groups. The struggles and accomplishments of handicapped individuals should be demonstrated and discussed. At its essence, gender-fair teaching should highlight and celebrate the rich diversity that comprises contemporary society.

4. Gender-Fair Teaching Should Be a Partnership among Teachers, Parents, and Community Members

Changing the stereotypes that close off children's aspirations and options is not easily accomplished. It needs the help and cooperation of others who care about the well-being and positive potential of children. You may need to form a partnership with parents and work closely with them. In communities with parents who are resistant and even hostile, you may have to explain to them what gender-fair teaching is about and why it is an important educational issue. Show them the facts and figures. Explain how gender-fair teaching may actually work toward improving boys' achievement scores in reading and girls' achievement scores in math. When parents are already concerned about the impact of sexism on their children, enlist this important resource in an active teaching partnership. Explain to the parents what you are doing in your classroom so they can reinforce these lessons at home. Some of these parents may themselves be involved in nonstereotyped careers and life-styles. They, as well as other community members, may want to come into your classrooms to talk about their occupations and their experiences.

5. Gender-Fair Teaching Is a Total Process--It Should Involve All Aspects of the Classroom Environment

Gender-fair teaching involves the physical arrangement and organization of your room; verbal and nonverbal classroom language and interaction; selection and use of print and audiovisual curricular materials; and development of classroom lessons, units, and learning centers.

Every aspect of the classroom environment will teach children about roles and options for females and males, and students are sensitive to inconsistencies. For example, if you include women who have made outstanding achievements in your social studies lessons but fail to represent women in bulletin board displays, students will be aware of the incongruity. If you talk about the importance of women and men working together but allow segregation in classroom groups, lines, and other activities, students will be confused by this contradiction. All aspects of the classroom should consistently reinforce the message that equal educational opportunity is a reality for all students.

6. Gender-Fair Teaching Is Good Teaching

Enthusiasm, humor, creativity, patience, careful planning, flexibility, and respect for diverse student opinions are some of the qualities that characterize good teaching, and they are essential for effective gender-fair teaching. There are many obstacles to nonsexist teaching, including parent and student misunderstanding and resistance. But research on gender-fair instructional interventions shows that highly skilled and enthusiastic teachers can overcome these obstacles and help both boys and girls become less gender biased in their attitudes and behaviors (23).

7. Gender-Fair Teaching Must Include Both the Affective and Cognitive Domains

Students usually have strong feelings about the appropriate behavior and roles for women and men. Consequently, gender-fair instruction must help students examine and understand their ideas, attitudes, and feelings. For example, one student read a U.S. Department of Labor summary of facts and statistics concerning the increasing participation of women in the salaried work force. His attitude, " a woman's place is in the home," was so strong that he refused to believe the statistics; the facts denied reality as he wished reality to be. After participating in value-clarification activities on changing roles for men and women, the student was able to consider information on working women in a more intellectually open manner.

8. Gender-Fair Teaching Is Active and Affirmative

Because students are bombarded with sexist messages and signals, nonsexist teaching must be an active and intentional process of incorporating into daily instruction those books, audiovisual materials, discussions, research projects, field trips, enrichment activities, learning centers, and lesson plans and units that teach girls and boys about changing roles and widening options. In short, it is not enough to have a classroom library that includes gender-fair books. It is not enough to bring in nontraditional role models on career awareness day and to refer to "firefighters" instead of "firemen." These steps are all good and positive but they are not enough. In order to effect change for your students, in order to help them question and condemn prejudice on the basis of sex you will need to include examples, references, lesson plans, and learning-center ideas every day in your discussions and assignments.

At this point you may be thinking that this is a naive, idealistic recommendation, and that with all the other problems there is no time for such an active and all-encompassing approach. After all, there are more pressing problems to worry about such as achievement scores and back-to-basics. But if you are tempted to dismiss this recommendation, remember that there is nothing more basic than equal opportunity for all your students.

References

1. Association for Intercollegiate Athletics for Women. AIAW School Year Summary, 1978-79. Washington, D.C., 1979.

2. Bem, S. The Measurement of Psychological Androgyny. Journal of Consulting and Clinical Psychology 42. pp. 155-162. 1974.

3. Bem, S. Sex Role Adaptability: One Consequence of Psychological Androgyny. Journal of Personality and Social Psychology 31. pp. 634-643. 1975.

4. Britton, G., and Lumpkin, M. A Consumer's Guide to Sex, Race, and Career Bias in Public School Textbooks. Corvallis, Oregon: Britton and Assoc., 1977.

5. Brophy, J., and Good, T. Feminization of American Elementary Schools. Phi Delta Kappan 54, pp. 564-566. April 1973.

6. Caplan, P. Sex, Age, Behavior, and School Subject as Determinants of Report of Learning Problems. Journal of Learning Disabilities 10, pp. 314-316. May 1977.

7. Casper, W. An Analysis of Sex Differences in Teacher-Student Interaction as Manifested in Verbal and Nonverbal Behavior Cues. Ph.D. dissertation, University of Tennessee, 1970.

8. Child, I., Potter, E., and Levine, E. Children's Textbooks and Personality Development: An Explanation in the Social Psychology of Education. Psychological Monographs 60. 1946.

9. Davis, W. A Comparison of Teacher Referral and Pupil Self-Referral Measures Relative to Perceived School Adjustment. Psychology in the Schools 15, pp. 922-926 January 1978.

10. Duke, D. Who Misbehaves? A High School Studies Its Discipline Problems. Educational Administration Quarterly 12, pp. 65-85. Fall 1976.

11. Dweck, C., and Gilliard, D. Expectancy Statements as Determinants of Reactions to Failure: Sex Differences in Persistence and Expectancy Change. Journal of Personality and Social Psychology 32, pp. 1077-1084. 1975.

12. Dweck, C., and Reppucci, N. Learned Helplessness and Reinforcement Responsibility in Children. Journal of Personality and Social Psychology 25, pp. 109-116. 1973.

13. Etaugh, C. and Harlow, H. Behaviors of Male and Female Teachers as Related to Behaviors and Attitudes of Elementary School Children. The Journal of Genetic Psychology 127, pp. 163-170. 1975.

14. Eversoll, D. The Changing Father Role: Implications Parent Education Programs for Today's Youth. Adolescence 14, pp. 535-544. Fall 1979.

15. Felsenthal, H. Sex Differences in Expressive Thought of Gifted Children in the Classroom. American Educational Research Association, ERIC, Ed. 039-106, 1970.

16. Fling, S., and Manosevitz, M. Sex Typing in Nursery School Children's Play Interests. Developmental Psychology 7, pp. 146-152. September 1972.

17. Fox, L. The Effects of Sex Role Socialization on Mathematics Participation and Achievement. In Women and Mathematics: Research Perspectives for Change, L. Fox, E. Fennema, and J. Sherman, NIE Papers in Education and Work, No. 8. Washington, D.C.: National Institute of Education, 1977.

18. Frazier, N., and Sadker, M. Sexism in School abd Society. New York: Harper & Row, 1973.

19. Gillespie, P., and Fink, A. The Influence of Sexism on the Education of Handicapped Children. Exceptional Children 41, pp. 152-162. November 1974.

20. Goldberg, H. The Hazards of Being Male. New York: Nash, 1976.

21. Goldman, W., and May A. Males: A Minority Group in the Classroom. Journal of Learning Disabilities 3, pp. 276-278. May 1970.

22. Good, T. and Brophy, J. Questioned Equality for Grade One Boys and Girls. Reading Teacher 4, 25:247-52. 1971.

23. Guttentag, M., and Bray, H. Undoing Sex Stereotypes: Research and Resources for Educators. New York: McGraw-Hill, 1976.

24. Hartley, R. Sex Role Pressures and the Socialization of the Male Child. Psychological Reports 5. 1979.

25. Jourard, S. The Transparent Self. New York: Van Nostrand, 1976.

26. Komarovsky, M. Dilemmas of Masculinity: A Study of College Youth. New York: Norton, 1976.

27. Kuhn, D., Nash, S., and Bricken, L. Sex Role Concepts of Two and Three-Year-Olds. Child Development 49, pp. 445-451. June 1978.

28. Leinhardt, G., Seewald, A., and Engel, M. Learning What's Taught: Sex Differences in Instruction. Journal of Educational Psychology 71, pp. 432-439. August 1979.

29. Lietz, J., and Gregory, M. Pupil Race and Sex Determinants of Office and Exceptional Educational Referrals. Education Research Quarterly 3. Summer 1978.

30. Maccoby, E., and Jacklin, C. The Psychology of Sex Differences. Stanford, California: Stanford University Press, 1974.

31. Mullis, I. Educational Achievement and Sex Discrimination. Denver: National Assessment of Educational Progress, 1975.

32. National Assessment of Educational Progress. Reading Change, 1970-75: Summary Volume. Reading Report No. 06-R-21. Denver: National Assessment of Educational Progress, 1978.

33. Nicholls, J. Casual Attributions and Other Achievement-Related Cognitions: Effects of Task Outcomes, Attainment Value, and Sex. Journal of Personality and Social Psychology 31. 1975.

34. Olsen, N., and Willemsen, E. Studying Sex Prejudice in Children. The Journal of Genetic Psychology 133, pp. 203-216. December 1978.

35. Pleck, J., and Brannon, R. Male Roles and the Male Experience. Journal of Social Issues 34. 1978.

36. Sells, L. High School Mathematics as the Critical Filter in the Job Market. In Developing Opportunities for Minorities in Graduate Education. Proceedings of the Conference on Minority Graduate Education at the University of California, Berkeley. 1973.

37. Serbin, L., and O'Leary, D. How Nursery Schools Teach Girls to Shut Up. Psychology Today 9, pp. 57-58 and 102-103. 1975.

38. Smith, S. Age and Sex Differences in Children's Opinion Concerning Sex Differences. Journal of Genetic Psychology 54. March 1939.

39. Stone, P. Child Care in Twelve Counties. In The Use of Time, Alexander Szalai (ed.). The Hague: Mouton, 1972.

40. U.S. Commission on Civil Rights. _More Hurdles to Clear_. Washington, D.C., 1980.

41. U.S. Department of Labor. Women's Bureau. _The Earnings Gap Between Men and Women_ 1979; _Twenty Facts on Working Women_, 1978.

42. U.S. Department of Labor. Women's Bureau 1980-1984 statistics.

43. Waldron, J. Why Do Women Live Longer than Men? _Journal of Human Stress_ 2. 1976.

44. Wirtenberg, T. Expanding Girls' Occupational Potential: A Case Study of the Implementation of Title IX's Anti-Segregation Provision in Seventh Grade Practical Arts. Ph.D. dissertation, University of California, 1979.

45. Women's Equity Action League. _Facts about Women in Education_. Washington, D.C. 1976.

Sexism in Education

Members of a New Guinea tribe studied by anthropologist Margaret Mead in the early 1930s believed that only a baby born with its umbilical cord wrapped around its neck would grow up to be an artist. Astoundingly, such babies did grow up to become artists. And no matter how hard and long other tribe members practiced, they never became accomplished artists (21). Social expectations for adult development in this tribe had clearly limited the achievement possible for individual tribe members.

Is it possible that in enlightened twentieth-century America we limit individual achievement in the same way by delineating roles, jobs, and behavior based on arbitrary factors such as sex, race, and social class? Educators, parents, and politicians claim that they want every individual to have access to all opportunities afforded by this society. But beneath this professed philosophy there seems to run a deeper current of assumptions that the capacities, interests, and talents of people are related to their class, color, and sex. Much like the accidental placement of the umbilical cord, these factors subtly influence an individual's possibilities for adult achievement.

This difference between our stated philosophies of education and our actual expectations for student achievement accounts for the mixed messages children receive in school.

They are told that they can be anything they want to be and that all opportunities, careers, and life styles will be available to them as adults. In practice, however, subtle factors work to result in the sorting, grouping, and tracking of minority and female students in stereotyped patterns that prepare them to accept traditional roles and jobs in adult life, rather than to explore all options and opportunities according to their individual talents and interests.

These subtle influences on students are part of the unplanned, unofficial learning that children absorb as they move through school--often called the hidden curriculum. This hidden curriculum includes the messages children receive about themselves and others of their sex and race through the illustrations, language, and content of textbooks, films, and visual displays; the ways in which administrators, teachers, and other students interact with them; the part they play in important school rituals; and the extent to which they come in contact with influential role models of their own sex and race.

Thus, poor, minority, and female students learn very early that social expectations for their development limit them to traditional educational and career patterns. On the other hand, affluent, nonminority, male students find that society has high expectations for their performance and achievement and that anything less represents failure. Fortunately, our educational and social systems are flexible enough to allow people to try out and succeed in nontraditional paths. We all know many persons who have surmounted the handicaps of arbitrary and limiting social expectations.

As educators, your role is to ensure that your students break away from group stereotypes to explore and pursue a wide variety of school and life options. You will be strengthening individual students to resist the continuous influx of messages about sex-, race-, and class-appropriate roles, jobs, and behaviors.

You have the opportunity to break the vicious circle that may otherwise imprison your students for the rest of their lives. This vicious circle is a web of attitudes and behaviors that severely restricts options for human development. In prescribing what is appropriate and natural for people based on their class, sex, and race, it functions as a self-fulfilling prophecy.

The vicious circle of sexism begins with commonly accepted stereotypical assumptions regarding sex differences. These assumptions manifest themselves in different expectations for and treatments of girls and boys in school. When students undergo different experiences, training, and opportunities based on their sex, they lose their individual academic, occupational, and personality potential. As adults, these well-rehearsed students take up traditional functions at home, at work, and in the community. The perpetuation of these traditions reinforces stereotyped assumptions people hold about what is appropriate and natural for women and men, and the circle of sexism continues.

Sex Discrimination Today? Don't Be Ridiculous!

In early American society women were not considered the equals of men. They were not sent to school or permitted to vote, had no legal control over their property or children, could not initiate a divorce, and could not smoke or drink in public. These facts sound like ancient historical curiosities, as outdated as pantaloons and powdered wigs. Today, few people think there is any difference between the way women and men are treated, especially in school.

Certainly, most teachers, counselors, and principals do not want to be guilty of sexual or racial discrimination or of discrimination based on a person's physical or emotional handicap. They want to treat students as unique individuals.

But regardless of well-stated philosophies of education, people act on the basis of deep-rooted assumptions that differentiate between the appropriate behaviors, roles, and jobs for women and men. These assumptions may not even be conscious, but they result in subtle differences in the ways people are treated--what we expect from them, how we think they should act, how we think they should look, and how we think they should respond to us.

Assumption 1: A Woman's Place Is in the Home

Conventional wisdom. Many people today believe that a woman should have job skills in case she must work. Her primary prescribed role, however, is in the home; if in the paid work force, it should be as a nurturer, helper, and supporter.

Implications for schooling. If women are to orient themselves around the home rather than around civic or economic affairs, then they must be reinforced with domestic images and goals. If women are to be mothers, elementary-school teachers, secretaries, nurses, hairdressers, maids, and social workers, then they do not need training in calculus, physics, chemistry, auto mechanics, or welding. If a young woman is to concentrate on catching a husband, then it is not necessary for her to plan seriously for college or a career.

Assumption 2: Women Are Physically, Emotionally, and Intellectually Inferior to Men

Conventional wisdom. Human history, as recorded in history books, subtly communicates the idea that women have contributed little to society except babies. They have not been hunters, builders, explorers, artists, leaders, scholars, or philosophers. This is evidence to many people of the inferior physical, emotional, and intellectual makeup of women. A tradition of protection has arisen for this supposedly poorly endowed but necessary group--protection from strenuous physical exertion, protection from stress, protection from unpleasantness, protection from fiscal matters, protection from decision making, protection from competition, and protection from intellectual challenge.

Implications for schooling. If strenuous activity, physical exertion, and competition are not appropriate for women, then rigorous physical education programs and interscholastic team sports are not essential. If women are emotionally fragile, then they ought not be given leadership responsibilities in classes or clubs. If women are not intellectual, then it is not essential that they master highly complex information--particularly in areas of politics, science, and technology.

Assumption 3: Women Should Cultivate Traditionally Feminine Characteristics

Conventional wisdom. Many people find ambitious, decisive, challenging, independent, or intellectual women to be unfeminine and offensive. They want women to develop their talents but to remain typically feminine--deferential, accommodating, restrained, and accepting. Women who adopt conventionally male modes of behavior are often mocked, scorned, or pitied.

Implications for schooling. If women are to exhibit typically feminine behaviors, then they must be reinforced for being attractive, sweet, quiet, attentive, and neat; not for being scholarly, questioning, argumentative, or independent. Inappropriate behavior such as physical and intellectual assertiveness can be discouraged through ridicule, lack of attention, or punishment.

If Amelia Earhart Had Been a Lady, She Wouldn't Have Had Wings

As a child, Amelia Earhart, the well-known aviator who made a solo flight across the Atlantic Ocean one year after Charles Lindbergh, was encouraged to experiment, to build things, to run free and explore the outdoors along with her brothers. Her husband, in his biography of her, traces her "masculine" spirit of adventure to this "deviant" upbringing (3). Many outstanding women remember being tomboys as children.

Successful adults in our society, men and women both, exhibit the "masculine" characteristics independence, assertiveness, ability to lead, self-reliance, and emotional stability. Are schools nurturing these traits in female students?

In the nineteenth century, affluent families sent their daughters to female academies where they learned the skills necessary to make a good marriage: foreign languages, piano, handwriting, embroidery, religious reading. Girls and boys in today's schools are not assigned separate curricula; they have exposure to the same experiences and training. Is it possible that despite this progress toward equal education we are still subtly preparing girls primarily for marriage and motherhood and a few traditional career goals? Alvin Toffler writes in Future Shock, "Our schools face backward toward a dying system rather than forward to the emerging new society" (40). Is the nineteenth-century view of women still with us?

Vehicles of Differential Treatment

Certain traditional vehicles exist through which educators transmit the information, skills, and experiences believed necessary for students. These vehicles include textbooks and other instructional materials, the curriculum, teacher behavior, counseling materials and techniques, physical activity, and extracurricular activities.

As these traditional educational vehicles prepare students for adult life in this society, they also communicate subtle but powerful messages about appropriate female and male roles, jobs, and behaviors.

Textbooks and Instructional Materials

Can you imagine school without textbooks? Was there ever a year you did not have a stack of those heavy, hardcover books with the slick paper from which classroom lessons were conducted and homework assigned? You probably carried them around, did your assignments, read aloud from them in class without ever consciously noticing the sexual, racial, ethnic and class biases they reflected. From those books you learned reading, mathematics, history, literature, science, and psychology.

While you were learning the cognitive information conveyed in those books, you were also assimilating the latent biases. Textbooks appear to be authoritative and are treated with reverence by many teachers. Thus we tend to absorb the subtle messages they convey (through language, illustrations and content) without questioning the information that is omitted, included, and how that information is arranged.

The hidden messages in textbooks have been analyzed by a number of researchers. Their findings are startling and unsettling because we have grown up oblivious to these subtle but pervasive messages.

The participants of a major study conducted in 1972, the results of which appear in Dick and Jane as Victims, analyzed 2,760 stories in 134 elementary-school readers published by fourteen United States publishing companies. They reported the following ratios (47):

Boy-centered to girl-centered stories 5:2
Adult male to adult female main characters 3:1
Male to female biographies 6:1
Male to female animal stories 2:1
Male to female folk or fantasy stories 4:1

This study found that the males portrayed in these stories demonstrated the traits of ingenuity, creativity, bravery, perseverance, achievement, adventurousness, curiosity, sportsmanship, helpfulness, skill acquisition, competitiveness, power use, autonomy, self-respect, and friendship. These males also displayed the attitude that anything associated with femininity is unmanly and is to be avoided at all costs.

Girls in these stories demonstrated the traits of dependency, passivity, incompetence, fearfulness, concern about their physical appearance, obedience, domesticity. "Little girls endlessly play with dolls, cry over dolls, give tea parties, look on helplessly or passively or admiringly while boys take action... They look on while boys play cowboy, look on while boys make carts, look on while boys rescue animals, look on while boys save the day" (48).

In a study of illustrations in science, math, reading, and social studies textbooks published between 1967 and 1972, females comprised only 31 percent of the total illustrations (although they are 51 percent of the population) and as the grade level increased, the number of pictures of females decreased. Minority women were pictured one-half as often as minority men, who were themselves inadequately portrayed (45).

A 1971 study of women in more than twelve of the most popular U.S. high school history textbooks found that women were omitted from the topics discussed and, when portrayed at all, were in passive roles (41). Male figures were featured and quoted almost exclusively. Male pronouns ("he," "his") were used to refer both to men and to women, implying that all historical activities were carried on by men. The texts surveyed demonstrated that the contributions made by American women to colonial life, the Civil War, frontier life, and the world wars were overlooked. Also omitted were women's work on pioneer farms, the role of women in the earlier days of the labor movement, the development of birth control and its impact on the American family, and the issues of sex discrimination in society.

Sex stereotyping and bias have also been found to be pervasive in other instructional materials on which teachers depend: audiovisual aids of all types, paperback books, individualized learning kits, curriculum units, and tests.

In response to pressures for change, many publishers have developed nonsexist guidelines for their authors. However, although some changes are evident in more recently published texts, bias remains. A review of more recent studies on sexism in children's reading materials (1975, 1976, 1977), some of which are replications of earlier studies, concludes that progress toward nonsexist books is slow. For example, a 1972 study found 84 percent of the women shown in homemaking roles and 17 percent in professional roles. In the 1975 replication study, 68 percent of the women were in homemaking roles and 32 percent in professional roles (39). Although change has occurred, the books are still biased.

A recent study reports similar findings for university texts. An analysis of the twenty-four most widely used teacher education texts found that twenty-three give less than 1 percent of their space to the issue of sexism. One-third do not mention the issue of sexism at all. Most of the texts guilty of this oversight are in math and science--the areas in which girls are most likely to have achievement difficulties. Not a single text provides future teachers with curricular resources and instructional strategies to counteract sexism in the classroom and its harmful impact on children (31).

Curriculum

When we speak of the curriculum of a school we refer to the plan of study for the students in that school during their enrollment there. This includes the courses they take, the description and content of those courses, and the methods by which they are taught. It also includes the educational tracks students follow--general, academic, business, vocational.

Until recently there was a variety of single-sex courses offered in high schools around the country: powder-puff football, bachelor cooking, girls' and boys' physical education. Some classes were required of each sex for graduation, such as home economics for girls and shop for boys. Course descriptions, language, and content have often made it abundantly clear that no students of the other sex were welcome: "This course in sewing is for the student who would like to make some of her own clothes."

Course content and methodology frequently make it difficult for students of one sex to relate to the subject matter. Sex-biased language, assignments, activities, and tests perpetuate traditional stereotypes. We forget that tests teach as well as assess. For example, a test question might read: In the United States, voters do not directly choose the man they wish to be president. This, of course, reinforces the notion that women are not suited for the presidency.

The contributions by women and minorities are frequently ignored or treated superficially no matter what the subject may be. This conveys the impression that the only worthwhile contributions to our history and culture have been made by white males.

Course prerequisites may be discriminatory if one sex has been discouraged or prevented from taking required courses or training. Discrimination also exists when students must choose from sex-stereotyped units or classes such as modern dance and basketball.

Students enter educational tracks--general, academic, business, vocational--based on counseling, teacher recommendation, vocational and achievement testing, peer and parental pressure, personal interest, and tradition. Curriculum ghettos exist in many schools as students continue to make choices based to a great extent on race, sex, and class expectations. These choices will have enormous impact on their adult lives. For example, white girls predominate in typing and shorthand classes; thus it is unlikely that boys or minority girls will get clerical or secretarial jobs. Because white boys predominate in trade courses, girls and minority boys are not prepared for jobs in welding, carpentry, and auto mechanics.

The courses students take in secondary school influence and limit subsequent college and career choices. Most girls, for example, do not go on for advanced science and mathematics classes even if they do well in those subjects. Although there is no difference in the ability of males and females to do mathematics, there is an enormous gap in the number that study mathematics. Lacking four years of college-preparatory math, young women find themselves eliminated from many college majors, including astronomy, civil engineering, biochemistry, physics, mathematics, medicine, forestry, economics, and computer science. Thus, they generally find themselves in education, social work, nursing, and the humanities--fields that offer much in the way of social worth, but at comparatively lower pay.

Nor is it that boys like mathematics better than girls do. In a study of secondary-school students, one researcher found no difference in the degree to which female and male students liked mathematics relative to other subjects (28). The greater participation by males in math is related instead to their understanding that math may be a necessary prerequisite for their subsequent careers.

Although black girls are more likely to have to work than white girls, 58 percent of black high school girls as compared with 44 percent of white high school girls enroll in the general curriculum, which offers little skill training, rather than a vocational, college preparatory, or commercial program. Among young black women out of school, those who had enrolled in the general curriculum experienced the most unemployment (37).

Vocational education is a training ground for the world of work. However, nearly one-half of all girls enrolled in vocational education are in consumer and homemaking courses, which prepare them for very few paying jobs. Moreover, the courses of study that do train for employment, and in which girls predominate, offer training in only thirty-three different occupations. In contrast, courses of study in which boys predominate offer training for paid employment in ninety-five different occupations. When girls do enroll in programs leading to paid employment, it is most often in areas such as office or health services education, which offer relatively poor pay and relatively poor prospects for advancement (44). Minority females seem to be disproportionately concentrated in those areas of training for which anticipated pay is lowest.

Boys tend to enroll in agriculture and skilled-trades programs, girls in home economics, child-care, fashion-merchandising, office-occupation, and cosmetology programs. Since 1972, there has been an increase of 10 percent more boys studying home economics, but less than 1 percent more girls in trade and industrial programs.

Teacher Behavior

As you think back over your school experiences, you may remember one or two teachers who made a difference in your life. Why were those teachers significant to you? Was it that they made you feel good about yourself, special, important, worthwhile? Was it that they pushed you to study and learn, believing in your ability to master the subject matter? Was it that they found out what you were good at and rewarded you for it?

Many children do not receive that kind of support and encouragement from any of their teachers. The basic assumptions teachers hold about people influence the messages they convey to their students. Teachers in mixed-school settings interact more with high-achieving, white, male students. When questioned, most teachers prove to be unaware of such bias in their behavior and appalled at the idea of it. However, research indicates that teachers do have different sets of expectations, behavior standards, rewards, and punishments for female and male students, minority and nonminority students, high and low achievers. Other manifestations of teacher bias can be found in classroom assignments, course content, materials, activities, language, tests, displays, and class groupings based on sex and race.

From the moment boys enter school, most teachers expect them to be noisy, aggressive, sloppy, poor at reading, and good at mathematics. Teachers also tend to expect girls to be well behaved, quiet, neat, good at reading, and poor at mathematics. One researcher investigated the effect of teachers' beliefs on pupil achievement and concluded that if teachers believe that first-grade boys will do as well in reading as girls do, then this will happen. Conversely, if teachers do not expect boys to do as well as girls, then their reading performance will be lower (26). In our nation's schools boys more often than girls demonstrate reading and other learning difficulties; this is not true in other countries where such problems are not sex-linked and teachers expect boys to be good readers (1).

In one study, junior high school teachers were asked to select adjectives that they thought would describe good male and good female students (16). Their responses are shown in Table 1.

Table 1
Adjectives Used by Junior High School Teachers to Describe Good Male and Female Students

Good Male Students	Good Female Students
Active	Appreciative
Adventurous	Calm
Aggressive	Conscientious
Assertive	Considerate
Curious	Cooperative
Energetic	Dependable
Enterprising	Efficient
Frank	Mannerly
Independent	Mature
Inventive	Obliging
	Poised
	Sensitive
	Thorough

Other studies indicate that many teachers have lower expectations for black students than for whites and give less attention to black students (30).

Research with elementary-school teachers indicates that they interact far more with boys than with girls. Boys are not only reprimanded more, but they also receive more praise, and more direct instruction; they are listened to more frequently, and are rewarded more for creative behavior (32).

The kinds of tasks and groupings assigned by teachers are often based on stereotyped notions about appropriate female and male behavior. Boys are asked to carry books, move furniture, operate audiovisual equipment; girls are asked to carry messages and erase the chalkboard. Girls in elementary school are frequently bigger and stronger than boys, but they are protected from such arduous chores as carrying books. Because of their assumed mechanical ineptitude, they do not have opportunities to operate complicated machinery like film projectors.

Many teachers continually reinforce what they perceive to be innate, appropriate, and irreversible sex differences. This creates animosity and competition between female and male students. Spelling bees and debates pit girls against boys. Girls and boys are grouped separately for projects. A girl who shoots spitballs might be shamed by the teacher who says, That's not ladylike behavior. I am ashamed of you! Boys who misbehave are often punished and humiliated by being sent to sit with the girls. In addition, for similar kinds of misbehavior, boys are more often physically punished than girls. And, minority students are subjected to more frequent disciplinary action than nonminority students.

Counseling and Guidance

Students may be influenced by a variety of school personnel when making course and career decisions--teachers, counselors, administrators, secretaries, and custodians. Guidance counselors, of course, do more formal course and career counseling than other school personnel. They are also responsible for most of the following activities: scheduling of classes; selection and interpretation of achievement, personality, and interest measurement tests; selection, display, and distribution of career guidance material; writing references; referring students to jobs.

These counseling activities play a primary role in sorting, classifying, and tracking students to fill socially prescribed occupational roles. Counselors, like teachers, often have different career expectations for females and males, and students can be greatly influenced by a counselor's attitudes about educational, career, and life choices. Two studies illustrate this point.

When female and male high school counselors were asked to listen to audiotaped self-descriptions of high school girls having either traditionally feminine or traditionally masculine goals, counselors of both sexes indicated that the "feminine" goals were more appropriate for female students and those girls with "masculine" goals were more in need of counseling services (38).

When asked to invent backgrounds and interests for college-bound and noncollege-bound women, male counselors portrayed college-bound women as interested in traditionally "female" occupations at the semiskilled level, while female counselors portrayed them as interested in occupations requiring a college education. In addition, male counselors did not consider any traditionally male careers for women (9).

Girls and boys today need counseling that is free from stereotyped expectations. For example, although 97 percent of all high school girls report that they expect to have careers, they are generally more interested in the arrival of Prince Charming and tend to underplan for their educational and occupational futures (24).

This vague, dreamy approach to their adult lives goes unchallenged by many counselors who fail to guide girls toward serious academic and career planning. Counselors, like other adults in education, are operating from the basic assumption that a girl's career will be her husband and not out-of-home work. These assumptions do not recognize that nine out of ten young women in today's high schools will work outside the home for the majority of their adult lives.

In general, tests and materials used by counselors to help students make academic and career choices also reflect traditional biases. Achievement tests have more references to men than to women, and show women primarily as homemakers or in pursuit of hobbies. Career-interest inventories offer a wider variety of career choices for males than for females and more careers at higher status and income. Materials describing careers often depict men in challenging professional or managerial positions. Many technical and trade brochures portray only males at work. And some college catalogs portray female and male students in stereotyped classes and roles.

Physical Activity

Physical-education classes and athletic programs offer students opportunities to develop strength, coordination, skills, good health habits, leisure-time pursuits, and teamwork. Physical development and fitness have a positive influence on intellectual and social development as well as on self-concept. Control over one's body in acts of skill promotes "the growth of an individual's sense of personal worth, self-reliance, personal freedom, and increases his [sic] worth as a social being" (7). Recently, researchers have confirmed that both male and female athletes are "less depressed, more stable and have higher psychological vigor than the general public (23).

Despite the knowledge that physical activity is good for people and despite the fundamental role played by sports in American culture, physical education and athletic programs from kindergarten through college minimize the importance of physical development for females. Girls have been treated as second-class citizens or worse in physical activities, relegated to separate and inferior classes, and to a few sports that receive nowhere near the level of equipment, facilities, staff, benefits, publicity, and money that boys' sports receive.

Physical ability varies more among individuals of the same sex than between the sexes, so segregation of students by sex for purposes of participating in physical activities is not an educationally sound method of grouping. Many girls are stronger, more skilled, and have more endurance than many boys. Good female athletes are praised by being compared to boys, as in, she throws just like a boy. Boys, on the other hand, are derogatorily compared to girls when they do badly, as in, Look at him, he runs like a girl! As a result of segregated classes and sports programs, which reflect different expectations and treatment based on sex, girls learn to view themselves as weaker than boys, more easily hurt, and they deduce from this that they are therefore inferior. Physical education has been called "the only sex-identified body of knowledge in the school curriculum" (42). (Imagine girls' social studies, or boys' English!)

From the time girls enter elementary school, they are discouraged from engaging in rowdy play or physical movement that is not "ladylike." Throughout their school years, girls receive a clear message about the value placed on their acquisition of athletic skills and strength. They are usually protected from strain or injury and prevented from developing skills and experiencing teamwork. The traditional feminine traits delicacy and physical weakness are reinforced, and girls are encouraged to participate in few athletics. Dancing, cheerleading, gymnastics, and pep squad have been the most acceptable outlets for them. More recently volleyball has been added as an acceptable female sport. Studies indicate that vigorous athletic programs and training are in no way injurious to females but, on the contrary, overprotectiveness inhibits the full development of their physical powers.

Are women interested in sports when given encouragement and opportunity? Between 1970 and 1979, the percentage of female high school athletes rose from 7 percent to over 30 percent. In some school districts, the number of girls participating in interscholastic athletics has risen over 600 percent since 1974.

The sex stereotyping that interferes with the development of girls works in the reverse for boys. If girls are not expected to enjoy and be good in sports, boys are expected to love and excel in athletics. Boys who do not are considered "sissies." All boys are encouraged, often forced, to participate in athletics from an early age. Continuous pressure on boys to compete and to win is very stressful, but athletic prowess brings prestige with peers and adult approval. The low- and average-ability male athlete is frequently overlooked by win-oriented sports programs.

Minority males and females face special problems. Black male students sometimes find acceptance and status through sports and dream of professional careers. Only a tiny percentage realize their dreams, and because schools fail to emphasize academic as well as athletic performance for black males, most find themselves with few career options.

Black females, on the other hand, are not rewarded for athletic participation. Opportunities and prestige at the high school are limited, and colleges offer far fewer athletic scholarships to women than to men. Minority female athletes who need financial aid to attend college are less likely than men to get it.

Sociologists point out that American business has been "socialized" by sports (29). "The road to the boardroom leads through the locker room," where boys learn loyalty, brotherhood, persistence, initiative, and sportsmanship. If women were allowed greater participation in competitive team sports, they would have more opportunities to develop the leadership and teamwork skills needed for managerial jobs.

Extracurricular Activities

Extracurricular activities have provided experiences and skills that reinforce basic assumptions about appropriate female and male roles, jobs, and behavior. Until recently this meant separate activities. Boys' activities have been oriented toward the development of creativity, leadership, and physical prowess. Males have traditionally dominated activities such as athletics, science clubs and competitions, aviation, photography, class clubs, marching bands, jazz bands, and student government. Many of these creative, intellectually stimulating, character- and leadership-building activities have been virtually off-limits to girls.

Girls' activities, on the other hand, have been designed to develop domestic skills and have focused on helping or serving others. Girls have been involved in cheerleading, pep squads, and future-teachers, future-homemakers, and service clubs. Until about 1975, a visitor to any high school in the United States would very likely have found the following classic division of activities: boys playing football and girls cheering; boys serving as student council president, girls as treasurer or secretary; boys in Future Farmers of America, girls in Future Homemakers; boys in the Key Club meeting important community leaders, girls as candy stripers at the local hospitals.

Many of these divisions have begun to break down and students have learned to work in mixed groups. This interaction and shared responsibility may overcome some of the awkwardness that arises when young men and women begin dating after the years of separation and hostility experienced as younger children.

We have seen how the traditional vehicles of education--instructional materials, curricula, teacher behavior, counseling, physical activity, extracurricular activities--are used to reinforce biased assumptions. What are the cumulative effects on girls and women of continuous bombardment by such messages? Are girls and boys being educated to cope with the realities of their adult lives?

Assessing the Damage

The characteristics cultivated in women are dependency, passivity, deference, sweetness, helplessness, agreeableness, weakness. Women tend to be low in self-esteem; ambivalent about success, power, and achievement; intellectually underdeveloped; unassertive; overeducated for the jobs they hold; underprepared for traditionally male careers; and at the bottom of the ladder in employment, status, pay, and advancement opportunity. These are generalizations about women as a group, of course, and do not apply to the many examples of successful, strong, assertive, independent women who have confounded the stereotypes.

The story of Emma Green follows. Everything that happens to Emma is true though Emma is not a real person but a composite of many women. Her story may read like a soap opera, but it is based on research about the rearing and education of girls. The story of Emma is told from a middle-class perspective because, unfortunately, most research on sex bias deals with middle-class subjects, most of them white. Many girls, however, those in the minority as well as in the majority, lower-class as well as middle-class, are to some degree captives of the same fairy tale. They believe that if they look pretty enough, smell good enough, and act sweet enough, they can catch a man who will protect and shelter them happily ever after.

Although 97 percent of high school girls today say they plan for salaried work, this is peripheral to their lives. They believe that their real rewards will come through their husbands and children. The Cinderella myth keeps girls from seriously planning educational and occupational goals. As you read this story, notice the messages Emma receives from her parents, teachers, counselors, and peers about appropriate female roles, jobs, and behavior. Notice that sometimes those messages come directly from the words and behavior of others and sometimes indirectly. Note also how these messages affect Emma.

The Story of Emma

Emma's parents would have preferred a son to carry on her father's family name; however, they soon adjusted to her arrival because she was a cute little girl. Her mother was rather pleased with a daughter. She felt that girls were neater, sweeter, and cleaner than boys--and more obedient. Girls, her mother knew, were helpful around the house because they could do chores and take care of younger brothers and sisters. As Emma grew up, she had dolls to play with, and tea sets, and doll houses; and girlfriends her age with whom to share these toys.

Once, when she was about to shinny up a tree, her father said, "No, Emma, don't do that. You might fall down and hurt yourself." The boys on her block were playing ball almost as soon as they could walk, and Emma used to watch them. Once or twice, she asked to play, but the boys said, "Ah, girls can't play ball. Go play with your dolls."

Within a few years Emma had a younger brother, Tom. Emma's father was proud to have a boy, and tossed him up in the air, and called him "Tiger." Tom was allowed to run and jump and play ball and climb trees. Emma watched him.

Emma and Tom watched television together. They followed the adventures of Superman, Batman, Spiderman, the Hardy Boys, and the Smurfs. They saw boys and men save lives, help people, and swing between buildings. The men appeared to be very brave, adventuresome, courageous, and independent. Tom could dream of being like these male heroes someday, but Emma could not because women in these shows were usually helpless, and they did not do exciting things.

At nursery school, Emma played in the doll corner similar to the one she had at home. There was a block corner and a truck corner, but the teacher, who was a very nice woman, rarely went to the block corner or the truck corner herself, so it did not seem like a thing that women did, and Emma never went to play with the blocks or the trucks.

When she entered first grade, Emma felt good. She could read a little and knew her numbers. But the teacher praised Emma's clothes and her polite behavior. And when Emma turned her papers in, the teacher did not say much about her work, except to comment on how neatly she had written her assignments.

Emma loved to read. Besides her textbooks, Emma read books from the library. The books had few pictures of girls or woman; they were mostly about boys and men doing important things. Her math and science books had no pictures of girls at all. Emma decided that that was because math and science were subjects meant for boys. She thought that if she were smart she could probably be a teacher when she grew up.

One thing Emma hated was taking tests. She got very nervous because she was afraid she would not do well. Sometimes when she got a good grade, the kids teased her and called her "Smarty-pants." She was not sure she liked being smart.

In junior high school Emma decided that she was ugly and no boy would ever look at her. She imagined that she would never get married unless she did something about her appearance. She and her friends began experimenting with makeup and started to diet.

In high school, at last, a boy asked Emma to go out with him. Her mother gave her some advice: "Smile and listen to your date. Ask him questions about how he does all the things he does. Don't talk too much. Boys don't like girls who talk too much. And remember, be polite, sit with your legs together. Act like a lady."

As she progressed through high school, Emma made good grades. She was an A and B student, and she liked school. Since junior high, however, she was not doing as well as she used to do on the achievement tests, especially in math, science, and civics. She had been a good math student but dropped it because math was boring and did not seem important to her career goals.

Emma wondered whether she should go to college. Even though she had a good grade point average and liked school, she was not sure that she would do well in college. But her parents encouraged her to go. For one thing, they said, she would meet some nice boys there.

After she had been in college for a year, Emma began to think seriously about what she ought to do for a career. She had heard that there were opportunities in engineering for women. When she asked a counselor about it, she found that because she had dropped out of math in high school so early, she would have to take two years of math just to catch up. She thought it would be a waste of time and decided that she might as well major in English because she was good at it, loved to read, and wrote well.

In college, she met Joe and fell in love with him. When they got married, Emma dropped out and went to work so that Joe could finish school. Emma took a job as a clerk in an office. She did not have any typing or stenography skills, but she was bright and taught herself to type.

When Joe graduated, he took a job with a large company. Emma soon gave birth to a boy and later two girls. Emma was completely involved with her husband and family, but she was bothered because sometimes Joe seemed more interested in his work than he was in her.

When Emma was thirty-nine and Joe was forty, Joe divorced Emma. Emma was at a loss. She wondered how she had failed Joe and what she had done wrong in her marriage. For a while Joe paid alimony and child support, but then he remarried and started a new family. Soon after, the money stopped.

Emma realized that she would have to get a regular job. She had worked on and off as a part-time clerk, but she had no skills with which to build a career. She had not even learned stenography. She went to an employment agency and they sent her to work as a file clerk, back to a job like the one she had twenty years ago when she dropped out of college.

Did you recognize any of Emma's experiences? Have they happened to anyone you know? To what extent do you believe her experiences to be typical for women in this society? What differences are there in the messages received by women with different racial, ethnic, and class backgrounds?

Research about Women

Sex preference. In a study of 1,500 young married women and 375 of their husbands, women expressed a preference for boy children two to one, and their husbands preferred boys to girls by as much as three or four to one (15).

Play. Children spend 65 percent of their free time playing. Girls tend to play indoor games, while boys play in "larger, more open spaces farther from home [which] contributes to greater physical development and training for independence. Complicated rules and strategies for team sports prepare boys for competition in work situations and survival in bureaucratic organizations, while girls' play develops interpersonal relationships and empathetic skills" (2).

Tomboys. According to one researcher, for a girl to develop into an intellectual person, she must be a tomboy at some point in her childhood (20).

Television. Women are underrepresented in television programming and news, and minority women are nearly invisible. When portrayed, women are shown in stereotyped roles (46).

Nursery school. Teachers act and react in quite different ways to boys and girls. While they encourage aggression in boys, they encourage dependency in girls (34).

Teacher interactions. Teachers praise and scold girls and boys for very different kinds of behavior. Boys are reprimanded for misbehavior and praised for academic performance. Girls are more likely to be criticized for their academic performance, and praised for nonacademic qualities such as appearance, neatness, and politeness (6).

Achievement tests. At the age of nine, female and male performances on achievement tests in mathematics, science, social studies, and citizenship are nearly equal, while females outperform males in reading, literature, writing, and music. However, by the age of thirteen, females begin a decline in achievement, which continues through age seventeen and into adulthood. By adulthood, males outperform females in everything but writing and music (25).

Grades. Girls make much better high school grades than boys, in part because they follow the rules, are better behaved and neater. Despite their good grades, girls are less likely than boys to believe that they have the ability to do college work (4).

Mathematics. Fifty-seven percent of the male students entering the University of California at Berkeley in 1973 had four years of high school mathematics. Only 8 percent of the entering female students had four years of math. Because five of the twenty majors at Berkeley require calculus or statistics, 92 percent of the entering females were not even eligible to take these courses. Unless they took the classes needed to catch up, they were limited to the traditional women's fields: humanities, music, social work, elementary education, guidance, and counseling (33).

Self-esteem. Fewer high school girls than boys rate themselves above average in leadership, popularity in general, popularity with the opposite sex, and intellectual as well as social self-confidence (4).

Careers. Although more elementary-school girls today are beginning to consider a variety of careers, they are unable to describe specifically what having a career would be like. Boys, in contrast, are able to describe in detail the activities that might comprise their chosen careers (13).

Career commitment. Decline in career commitment has been found in girls of high school age. This decline has been related to their feelings that male classmates disapproved of a woman's using her intelligence (12).

Career planning. Given their academic ability, females tend to underplan their future occupational and educational goals compared to boys. For example, girls who anticipate working in low-status occupations have higher grade point averages than do boys who anticipate working in medium-status occupations (5).

Jobs. Of the women in the work force in March 1978, nearly 80 percent were in clerical, sales, service, or factory jobs. In professional positions, 60 percent of the women were noncollege teachers or nurses, while men tended to be lawyers, doctors, or college professors (43).

Alimony and child support. Alimony awards are made in only 14 percent of all divorces, and only half are collected regularly. Forty-four percent of divorced mothers are awarded child support, which typically covers less than one-half the support costs of the children and are also very difficult to collect (14).

These findings raise serious questions about the rearing and education of women. If the overt and covert messages with which women are inundated confine them to nineteenth-century roles and jobs and make the female achiever into an object of fear, scorn, or ridicule, then we are out of step with the demands placed on adult women in twentieth-century America.

The lives of women in the twentieth century are dramatically different from the lives of their mothers and grandmothers. The majority of American women today work outside the home. By the year 2000, well over half of the labor force will be female. Most working women are single, divorced, widowed, separated, or have husbands earning under seven thousand dollars a year. They earn three-fifths of what men earn for the same work, and minority women are most likely to be underpaid and underemployed.

Our educational system has responded very slowly to these contemporary social realities. Our schools have always had dual, somewhat contradictory functions to perform. They are supposed to be conservers of the status quo and also harbingers of change. It has been easier to keep the status quo than to change, and our schools do not yet seem to be ready to educate young people for the future that awaits them. Although we should be training girls to earn a living to lead, to manage money and power, we have not quite eliminated the image of the nineteenth-century Victorian woman--the quiet, delicate, and passive woman who "knows her place."

In the course of Emma Green's story, there were many points at which understanding adults could have encouraged her full physical and intellectual development, increased her self-confidence, and oriented her toward realistic and satisfying academic and career goals. As an educator, you have the opportunity to nurture the Amelia Earhart in every girl, for it is there. Encourage girls to be assertive, brave, daring, athletic, intellectual, independent, creative, and strong. Then they will be better able to deal with life as it is for women in the world today.

If Men Are in Charge, Can They Be in Trouble?

Many people resent the recent emphasis on bias and discrimination against girls and women. They point out that boys and men also suffer damaging consequences as a result of differential treatment. Others believe that because males (white) run the world and are in power, we should not feel sorry for them. They point to the differential treatment as providing white males the skills, knowledge, and characteristics necessary to get and keep power, and to ensure a certain level of income and status. Each of these assumptions carries with it many implications for how boys should be educated.

Assumption 1: Men Must Participate Directly and Lead in the Civic, Political, and Economic Affairs of the Society

Conventional wisdom. More and more men are assuming some of the responsibility for home and child care, often because their wives are working. But prevailing sentiment still assigns the "important" work of the world to men. Men must support families, run businesses and factories, provide vital professional services, and govern the community and the nation. Men are under continuing pressure to advance themselves: the senator to become president; the teacher to become principal; the auto mechanic to own the shop; the factory worker to become the foreman or the shop steward.

Implications for schooling. Clearly, if men are to enter the job market at the best level they can and advance to the highest point they can, they must be bombarded with images of men at work, dominant and successful. They must be well-grounded in academics to be prepared for a wide range of career choices, or they must be taught marketable vocational skills. Men must be encouraged to accept responsibility for leadership, decision making, and risk taking as they progress through school.

Assumption 2: Men Are Physically, Emotionally, and Intellectually Superior to Women

Conventional wisdom. Men are generally thought to be stronger, wiser, and emotionally more stable than women. All a man needs to achieve success is training, drive, and opportunity. His status is heightened by the acquisition of an attractive, supportive, dependent wife.

Implications for schooling. If men are to run the world, then their minds and bodies must be fully developed to meet the challenges of adult life. If a strong, healthy body, a competitive spirit, and the ability to work cooperatively within a group are vital to a man's success in life, then as many boys as possible should participate in team sports. If men are to make discoveries, invent things, and write great novels, then intellectual curiosity and creativity must be valued and encouraged. If they are to work in the paid labor force all of their adult lives, then they must be given marketable job skills or a strong academic background and encouraged and reinforced through class and school division of responsibilities.

Assumption 3: Men Should Cultivate Traditionally Masculine Characteristics

Conventional wisdom. Boys learn early that all things associated with femininity are to be shunned, lest they be called "sissy," "fag," "queer," or "gay." Accepting roles and jobs that are conventionally feminine is thought to demean men, and only men who have already proven their masculinity through sports, business, or military success can relax and step out of character occasionally. Rosie Grier, a football player, can do needlepoint because no one would dare laugh at him. Although contemporary male heroes in movies, television, and novels are increasingly sensitive, tender, and gentle, they are also without question strong, brave, decisive, and dominant.

Implications for schooling. If men are to shun feminine qualities and develop masculine characteristics, they must be positively reinforced only for "manly" behavior. Emotional control must be encouraged, which means that fear, anxiety, distress, even great joy, must be contained and not expressed. Aggression and fighting are to be expected as natural expressions of masculinity.

The Price

When females and males are treated differently in schools, the results are bad for both. The pressure on men to compete and succeed results in frustration and stress. Traits of tenderness, sensitivity, and emotionality are underdeveloped in males as are child-rearing and homemaking skills. Unrestrained aggressive behavior causes serious problems in schools and in society.

While it is true that the images, models, and experiences of leadership and success to which boys are exposed do provide many of them the strength, self-esteem, motivation, and skills to achieve mastery of their environment, the cost is high. Most men work constantly to build and preserve their "masculinity." This superman fixation includes sexual virility, personal bravery, adventuresomeness, physical strength, skill in sports, aggressiveness, exercise of power, control, and dominance. Because the performance of most boys can never match all of these superhuman expectations, many become maladjusted, low achieving, truant, delinquent, inattentive, and rebellious young adults.

This is the story of Joe Green, Jr., the man Emma married. Like the story of Emma it may seem melodramatic, but remember that Joe is a composite of research findings about the negative results of traditional role expectations for men. As you read the story, notice the direct and indirect messages Joe receives from his parents, teachers, counselors, and peers about appropriate male roles, jobs, and behavior. Note, too, the effects of those messages.

The Story of Joe

Joe, Jr. was the third child of the Greens. His father was overjoyed when, after two girls, a namesake was born. The proud father gave out cigars and invited his friends over to see the sturdy-looking baby wrapped in blue blankets. "Mary, wake up the baby and carry him out here so my friends can get a good look at him," Joe, Sr. would command.

Joe grew up playing with cars and trucks and blocks. He learned very early that his parents did not approve when he played dolls and house with his sisters. His mother teased him and sent him back to his own toys.

As he grew older, Joe played cops and robbers, space explorers, and football with other boys his age. Sometimes, Joe wanted to stay home alone and read, but his mother pushed him outside to play with the boys. If Joe came home crying after he had fallen off his bike or had been hit with a ball, his parents would tell him not to be a crybaby and send him back outside.

Joe hated to fight, but the guys called him "sissy" and "chicken" so he fought, but he was always afraid he would get hurt. If Joe's father heard that he had backed away from a fight, he would get angry and lecture him about being a man and standing up to bullies. Joe was sure that his father would have preferred a different kind of boy--tougher, braver, stronger.

Joe saw very little of his father who came home late and tired in the evening. On weekends his dad wanted to do his own chores and then relax, but once in a while they fished or played ball together. Those were special times for Joe. One summer, Joe's father built him a tree house, which the boys promptly made off-limits to all girls including Joe's sisters. Joe and his friends teased his sisters, called them names, and made fun of the way they walked and talked.

From the time Joe entered school, he was a behavior problem. Teachers liked him, but he was always talking, fooling around, or daydreaming. He was frequently scolded and punished. It made him feel bad, but he was not able to change; he found school boring.

Joe made many friends at school, all of them boys. He felt that girls were strange and different. They played silly games, giggled, whispered, and were always combing their hair. They did not tell jokes, or play sports, and were always goody-goodies in class. Joe could see that his teachers liked girls much better than boys. For one thing, Joe imagined that girls were smarter because they always won the spelling bees against the boys. Joe hated it when he was punished for rowdy behavior by having to sit with the girls at lunch. Even his best friends teased him.

In junior high school there was pressure to have a girlfriend. Joe was shy. He liked a quiet girl named Donna. He liked her for a whole year without ever talking to her except once to offer her a piece of gum--which she refused. He went to some school dances and hung around with a group of his friends. They rated all the girls. Joe planned and rehearsed a good opener: "Hi, would you like to dance?" But he did not approach anyone. He was afraid they would refuse him, because he was not tall and muscular like Dave, a terrific dancer like Harold, or funny like Jackson.

The only class Joe liked was physical education. He was not an outstanding athlete; he was too small and too fearful of getting hurt to really be a competitor, but he enjoyed sports anyway. The coach and the kids were angry when Joe fumbled a move, but generally he did all right.

When he got to tenth grade, a counselor asked him about his career plans. "Oh," he said, "I'm going to be a lawyer." "Not with these grades, you're not," he was told. Joe was told to shape up and to take a language, plenty of math, history, and English.

Joe was afraid he would not even do well enough to get into college. It was hard for him to discuss his fear of being a failure with anyone. He did not want his counselor to think he could not do the work, and he did not want to disappoint his parents. None of his friends seemed to worry very much about schoolwork, so he did not feel comfortable talking about it.

Joe began to have pain in his stomach; he lost his appetite, but he was too ashamed to tell his parents. It was his mother who finally found out and sent him to a doctor.

The doctor warned him that if he did not relax he would have an ulcer by the time he was twenty-one. He also told him that liquor would aggravate his stomach. Joe was embarrassed and wondered how the doctor had guessed that he was drinking.

Joe did all right in his high school classes--at least well enough to get into college. There was never any question about his going to college and preparing for a career. Joe's father often stressed the importance of earning a good living in order to support a wife and family.

In college he continued a pattern he had begun during his last year of high school. He dated many different girls to avoid serious involvement. His friends began to call him a Romeo, and he did not mind at all. It made him feel masculine and successful.

In his junior year, Joe began a serious relationship with Emma. He felt a tremendous sense of release because he could talk to her in a way he had never been able to talk to anyone. When he and Emma got married, he strongly believed that his role was to protect and care for her. It made him uncomfortable when she took a job to support him through college, and he vowed that he would be so successful in his career that she would never have to work again.

After graduation, Joe accepted a job with a large company because he thought it was a good opportunity. He worked hard to prove himself so that he could get ahead. This meant long hours, intense concentration, figuring out the politics of the firm, cultivating the right associates. It was a strain, and Joe's stomach pain recurred. He knew he should slow down, but did not want to appear unsociable or unambitious.

Joe had little time for his family. He and Emma had three children, but he began to drift apart from them. He found himself more and more involved in his job, and eventually he had an affair with a woman he met at work.

After his divorce from Emma, that relationship ended also and Joe found himself alone and without a sense of purpose. He had not received a promotion in several years, and felt that he was a failure at business as well as in his personal life. He was bored with his work, and often dreamed of what it might have been like to be a successful lawyer. With his financial obligations, he realized it was foolish even to think about a career change. Joe struggled with bouts of severe depression, but eventually he forced himself to focus on his work. After a while, he married again. He and his new wife had a baby and Joe found little time, money, or energy for his other family.

The story of Joe may read like a soap opera, but it is based on research about men's lives. Perhaps you know men who have gone through some of Joe's experiences. Do the men you know talk about their personal problems, anxieties, and failures? How relevant is Joe's story to the experiences of men with differing racial, ethnic, and class backgrounds?

Research about Men

Toys. Parents can tolerate girls playing with boys' toys but both mothers and fathers strongly discourage boys from playing with girls' toys or doing "girlish" things (18).

Fathers and sons. Fathers spend relatively little time with their sons and the relations between them are poorer than those between girls and their mothers or fathers. Fathers are perceived as punishing or controlling agents (11).

Aggression. Boys are encouraged by parents to be aggressive while girls are not. In addition, almost all of the models on television that encourage aggression are men, thereby encouraging boys to continue the aggression they learn from their parents (8).

Teacher discipline. Boys receive eight to ten times more prohibitory control messages from teachers than do girls. In addition, when teachers criticize boys, they are more likely to use harsh or angry tones than when they reprimand girls (22).

Grades. Among boys and girls of comparable intelligence quotient (I.Q.) boys are more likely to receive lower grades than girls. Even boys who score as well or better than girls on achievement tests are more likely to get lower grades in school (27).

Maladjustment. Far more boys than girls are maladjusted, low-achieving, truant, delinquent, inattentive, and rebellious. National delinquency rates are five times higher among boys than girls (35).

Athletics. Athletes learn toughness, independence, emotionlessness, insensitivity to pain, and they learn to focus on the concrete details and goals of winning. In high school, these masculine characteristics are valued and bring success in dating, but in college women prefer other personality traits--greater openness, sharing of feelings, more verbal communication, and sensitivity to moods. While in high school, nonathletes experience feelings of failure, inadequacy, inferiority and nonmembership in the world of their male peers (36).

Male friendship. Although men may report more same-sex friendships than women do, these friendships are not usually close or intimate. Self-disclosure is either very low or utterly lacking between males (17).

Role strain. Over 80 percent of male college seniors experience some form of role strain (mild to severe) in fulfilling role obligations (19). Compared to females, males experience a higher accident rate, a higher alcohol and drug abuse rate, a higher suicide rate, and a higher general mortality rate. One researcher asserts that "attempts to fulfill (male) role requirements result in anxiety, emotional difficulty, a sense of failure, compensatory behavior which is potentially dangerous and destructive, and stress which results in physical illness and premature death" (10).

The research and information on which the story of Joe Green is based raise serious concerns about the effects of rigid sex-role expectations for men in our society. What is the loss in human potential to each man as well as to society as a whole?

What You Can Do

We have looked into the classrooms, corridors, and gyms of American schools to uncover the ways in which students are treated differently based on their sex. We have examined the negative results of sex-differentiated treatment for both women and men. Following is a brief summary of five major points.

1. Social expectations for people based on their sex limit the development of their full potential.

2. Despite the fact that many people deny the existence of sex bias and discrimination in schools, children are bombarded with overt and covert messages about what they can be and do based on their sex.

3. Girls and boys need encouragement to explore nontraditional as well as traditional options.

4. The vehicles of education (the instructional materials, curriculum, the counseling, the physical activity, and the extracurricular activities) convey information to students about appropriate female and male roles, jobs, and behavior.

5. The negative effects of differential treatment of women include: lowered self-esteem, limited educational and career goals, inadequate vocational and career training, physical and intellectual underdevelopment, ambivalence about success and leadership.

Keep in mind the information we have examined, which indicates that an individual's developmental potential may be limited by rigid sex-role stereotypes. Traditionally defined female and male roles may not suit the realities of contemporary society. In today's complex and changing society, a healthy adult must be self-reliant and assertive as well as caring and sensitive. Both men and women will find it increasingly necessary to express the full range of human behavior instead of being restricted to that which is stereotypically feminine or masculine.

In an ideal world, Emma and Joe Green would have been encouraged to explore a wide range of behaviors and experiences. They would both have played with blocks and trucks as well as with dolls; they would have climbed trees and played football, jumped rope and played space explorers.

Joe would have been encouraged to play with girls as well as boys; he would have been given a doll to hold so that he could express tenderness and also prepare for the possibility of parenthood. Emma's teachers would have paid more attention to the quality of her work and less to her appearance, while Joe's teachers would have given him more support for sensitive and nurturing behavior.

Emma's counselors would have presented the realities of adult life to her and would have helped her with careful educational and career planning. Joe's counselors would have encouraged him to express his doubts and anxieties, and they would have helped him determine what his real interests and talents were.

And, perhaps, in our ideal world, Emma and Joe would have entered their marriage as two fully developed human beings; neither a burden on the other, each confident and independent yet at times vulnerable and dependent. They would have been equally satisfied with female or male children and would have shared home and child-rearing responsibilities.

As an educator, you can take some specific steps toward this ideal world now.

1. Examine your own attitudes and behavior continuously for sex bias and stereotyping.
2. Help sensitize others to these issues by sharing information and exchanging ideas.
3. Do not let biased or discriminatory behaviors go unchallenged.
4. Inform others about their rights.
5. Continue to inform yourself about the issue of sexism in education by reading the latest news, reports, and research findings in this field.
6. Challenge the years of habit and tradition that keep female and male students confined to prescribed roles.
7. Keep in mind that you can be a leader in the process of change. You can help make this a better world for future Emmas and Joes. You can make a real difference.

References

1. Brophy, J., and Good, T. Feminization of American Elementary Schools. Phi Delta Kappan 54, pp. 564-566. April 1973.

2. Child's Play: What Every Parent Needs to Know. Ms., pp. 22. February 1977.

3. Cited in L. Banner, Women in Modern America: A Brief History. New York: Harcourt, Brace, 1974.

4. Cross, P. College Women: A Research Description. Journal of National Association of Women Deans and Counselors 32. Autumn 1968.

5. Douban, E., and Locksley, A. Teenaged Boys and Girls Suffer Different--But Equally Serious Psychological Problems. ISR Newsletter 5. Summer 1977.

6. Dweck, C. Sex Differences in the Meaning of Negative Evaluation Situations: Determinants and Consequences. Paper presented at the Annual Meeting of the Society for Research in Child Development, Denver, Colorado, 1975.

7. Edwards, H. The Sociology of Sport. Homewood, Illinois: Dorsey Press, 1973.

8. Farrell, W. The Liberated Man. New York: Random House, 1975.

9. Friedersdorf, N. A Comparative Study of Counselor Attitudes Toward the Further Educational and Vocational Plans of High School Girls. Unpublished study, Lafayette, Indiana, Purdue University, 1969. Cited in Implementing Title IX and Attaining Sex Equity--The Counselor's Role. Washington, D.C.: Resource Center on Sex Roles in Education, 1977.

10. Harrison, J. Warning: The Male Sex Role May Be Dangerous to Your Health. Journal of Social Issues 34. 1978.

11. Hartley, R. Sex-Role Pressures and the Socialization of the Male Child. And Jill Came Tumbling After: Sexism in American Education, J. Stacey. New York: Dell, 1974.

12. Hawley, P. What Women Think Men Think. Journal of Counseling Psychology, pp. 193-199. Autumn 1971.

13. Iglitzin, L. A Child's Eye View of Sex Roles, Sex Role Stereotyping in the Schools. Washington, D.C.: National Education Association, 1973.

14. International Women's Year Commission Study. Cited in "Wives Get Short Shrift." The Miami Herald. October 31, 1977.

15. It's a Boy! The Miami Herald. January 25, 1978.

16. Kemer, B. A Study of the Relationship Between the Sex of the Student and the Assignment of Marks by Secondary School Teachers. Ph.D. dissertation, Michigan State University, 1965.

17. Komarovsky, M. Dilemmas of Masculinity. New York: Norton, 1976. Cited in Journal of Social Issues 34. 1978.

18. Lansky, L. The Family Structure also Affects the Model: Sex-Role Attitudes in Parents of Pre-School Children. Merrill-Palmer Quarterly 13, pp. 139-150. 1967.

19. Lewis, R. Emotional Intimacy Among Men. Journal of Social Issues 34. 1978.

20. Maccoby, E. Women's Intellect. In The Potential of Women, Farber and Wilson (eds.). New York: McGraw-Hill, 1963.

21. Mead, M. Sex and Temperament in Three Primitive Societies. New York: Dell, 1935.

22. Meyer, W., and Thompson, G. Teacher Interactions with Boys, as Contrasted with Girls. In Psychological Studies of Human Development, Kuhlens and Thompson (eds.). New York: Appleton-Century-Crofts, 1963.

23. Morgan, W. University of Arizona Sports Psychology Laboratory. Quoted in Time, June 26, 1978.

24. National Assessment of Educational Progress. Essay Task: A Women's Place Is (Where?). NAEP Newsletter June 1977.

25. National Assessment of Educational Progress. Males Dominate in Educational Success. NAEP Newsletter. October 1975.

26. Parlady, M. For Johnny's Reading Sake. Reading Teacher 22, pp. 720-729. May 1969.

27. Peltier, G. Sex Differences in the School: Problem and Proposed Solution. Phi Delta Kappan 50. November 1968.

28. Rappaport, K. Sexual Roles and Mathematical Expectations. The Math Journal 19. Fall 1978.

29. Riesmen, D. Harvard sociologist. Quoted in Time, June 26, 1978.

30. Rubovitz, P., and Maehr, M. Pygmalion Analyzed: Toward an Explanation of the Rosenthal-Jacobson Findings. Journal of Personality and Social Psychology 25. 1973. See also E. Leacock, Teaching and Learning in City Schools. New York: Basic Books, 1969.

31. Sadker, M., and Sadker, D. Beyond Pictures and Pronouns: Sexism in Teacher Education Textbooks. Washington, D.C.: Department of Education, Women's Educational Equity Act Program. 1980.

32. Sears, P., and Feldman, D. Teacher Interactions with Boys and with Girls. In And Jill Came Tumbling After: Sexism in American Education, J. Stacey (ed.). New York: Dell, 1974.

33. Sells, L. Mathematics--A Critical Filter. The Science Teacher 45, pp. 28-29. February 1978.

34. Serbin, L., and O'Leary, D. How Nursery Schools Teach Girls to Shut Up. Psychology Today 9, pp. 57-58 and 102-103. 1975.

35. Sexton, P. Schools Are Emasculating Our Boys. In And Jill Came Tumbling After: Sexism in American Education, Stacey, J. (ed.). New York: Dell, 1974

36. Stein, P., and Hoffman, S. Sports and Role Strain. Journal of Social Issues 34. 1978.

37. Stevenson, G. Counseling Black Teenage Girls. Occupational Outlook Quarterly 19. Summer 1974.

38. Thomas, A., and Stewart, N. Counselor Response to Female Clients with Deviate and Conforming Career Goals. Journal of Counseling Psychology 18, pp. 352-357. 1971.

39. Tibbetts, S. Sex-Role Stereotyping in Children's Reading Material: Update. Journal of the National Association for Women Deans, Administrators, and Counselors 42. 1979.

40. Toffler, A. Future Shock. New York: Random House, 1970.

41. Trecker, J. Women in U.S. History High-School Textbooks. In And Jill Came Tumbling After: Sexism in American Education J. Stacey (ed.). New York: Dell, 1974.

42. Ulrich, C. Schools and Physical Survival. Non-Sexist Education for Survival. Washington, D.C.: National Education Association, 1973.

43. U.S. Department of Labor Statistics. Cited in An Overview of Women in the Workforce. Washington, D.C.: National Commission on Working Women. Center for Women and Work. September 1978.

44. Verheyden-Hilliard, M. Cracking the Glass Slipper: PEER's Guide to Ending Sex Bias in Your Schools. Washington, D.C.: Project on Equal Educational Rights, 1977.

45. Weitzman, L., and Rizzo, D. Biased Textbooks. Washington, D.C.: Resource Center on Sex Roles in Education, 1974.

46. Window Dressing on the Set: Women and Minorities in Television. A Report of the U.S. Commission on Civil Rights. Washington, D.C.: U.S. Commission on Civil Rights, 1977.

47. Women on Words and Images. Dick and Jane as Victims: Sex Stereotyping in Children's Readers. Washington, D.C.: Resource Center on Sex Roles in Education, 1974.

48. Women on Words and Images. Look Jane Look. See Sex Stereotypes. In And Jill Came Tumbling After: Sexism in American Education, J. Stacey (ed.). New York: Dell, 1974.

How Fair Is Your Language?

It is important to overcome written forms of gender bias and to provide positive messages to students. For this reason, it is essential that each of us has a general knowledge of the forms of bias in written materials and that we continue to extend our skills in overcoming such forms of bias.

Forms of Bias

Much of our knowledge of gender bias in written communications began with studies of race and ethnic bias in textbooks and instructional materials. Studies of racial, ethnic, and gender bias have identified a number of similarities in the forms of bias and stereotyping. For this reason, it is useful to examine the forms biases take on the basis of race, gender, or national origin.

There are at least six forms of racial, ethnic and gender bias that may be found in written materials.

1. Exclusion and Invisibility

The most common form of bias in written communications is the complete or relative exclusion, in the contents and

---

Adapted from the brochure, "What Color Is Your Language?" and the training manual, Building Sex Equity in Vocational Education, developed by the Illinois State Board of Education/Department of Adult, Vocational and Technical Education.

the illustrations used in the communications of particular groups.

Research suggests, for example, that textbooks published prior to the 1960s largely omitted any consideration of black Americans within contemporary society, and indeed rendered blacks relatively invisible in accounts or references to America after Reconstruction. Illustrations found in vocational textbooks or career counseling materials may ignore minorities and present a distorted view of student populations and the world of work.

Many studies indicate that women, who constitute over 51 percent of the U.S. population, represent approximately 30 percent of the persons or characters referred to throughout textbooks in most subject areas. More recent studies indicate that the textbooks that are designed for use in vocational education courses, which are frequently sex segregated, exclude or omit members of one sex. Thus, males are likely to be omitted from home economics or secretarial textbooks, and females may be omitted from textbooks used in technical and agricultural courses. A study of recruitment materials for traditional male careers revealed that women were omitted in illustrations and that the materials did not make an effort to include women.

Each of these is an example of bias through exclusion or invisibility.

2. Stereotyping

When they are included in written communications, racial and ethnic minority group members, both male and female are often portrayed as having only one particular attribute, characteristic, or role. Some of the stereotypes most frequently seen in written communications include the portrayal of Asian-Americans only as laundrymen or cooks; the portrayal of Mexican-Americans only as migrant workers or laborers; the portrayal of women primarily in their role as mothers (and secondarily as nurses, secretaries, teachers, or flight attendants) and as passive, dependent persons defined solely in terms of their home and family roles; the portrayal of men in a wide variety of occupational roles (and only occasionally as husbands and fathers), and as strong, assertive persons defined primarily in terms of their occupational roles.

Even when minorities and women are included in other roles they may be stereotypically depicted as working with or serving only other members of the same minority group (black teachers working with black students) or the same sex (female teachers working with females), or they are shown working with colleagues of the same race, ethnic group, or sex.

Stereotyping may occur with a number of variables: physical appearance; intellectual attributes; personality characteristics; career roles; domestic roles; and social class and social placement (access to personal, social or institutional power or dominance).

3. Imbalance and Selectivity

Written materials perpetuate bias by presenting only one interpretation of an issue, situation, or group of people. This imbalanced account restricts students' or employees' knowledge of the varied perspectives that may apply to a particular situation. Through selective presentation of information, written communications may distort reality and ignore complex and differing viewpoints. As a result, students are taught little or nothing about the contributions, struggles, and participation of women and minorities in our society.

For example, references to Mexican-Americans may emphasize the difficulties of illegal immigration without discussing the contributions that such workers are making to federal taxes and the social security system, or the historical perspectives of Mexico's ownership of major parts of what are now the southwestern states of the United States. And achievements of outstanding women and minorities may be referenced without acknowledgment of the barriers they had to overcome in order to succeed.

4. Unreality

Many researchers have remarked on the tendency of writers to ignore facts that are unpleasant or that do not conform to the stated value system of white majority culture. Communications often ignore the existence of prejudice, racism, discrimination, exploitation, oppression, sexism, and intergroup conflict. Controversial topics are glossed over. This unrealistic coverage denies students the information they need to recognize, understand, and perhaps someday, overcome the problems within our society. Examples of this unreality are readily found.

Career-education and career-counseling materials that suggest that racial, ethnic, and sexual discrimination are things of the past make no effort to provide students with a realistic view of the discrimination that they may face in the world of work and in the broader society.

Students are provided information about the careers open to them, but they are not provided information about the pay they can expect or the opportunities for advancement.

The progress made by some members of minority groups is discussed without discussing the problems that are continuing to face large numbers of minority group members.

The progress women have made is discussed without indicating the continuing earnings gap between employed women and employed men.

Women are portrayed in the home without recognizing that a majority of adult women work outside the home.

5. Fragmentation and Isolation

Bias through fragmentation and isolation takes two primary forms. First, discussions of minority groups and women may be physically or visually fragmented or isolated and delivered only in separate chapters or sections (e.g., "Careers for Women," or "Economic Conditions of Black Americans"), or even in boxes to the side of the page (e.g., "Ten Distinguished Black Americans," "Women Labor Leaders"). Second, racial and ethnic minority group members and women may be depicted as interacting only with persons like themselves, never contacting or impacting the dominant culture.

Fragmentation and isolation imply that the history, experiences, and situations of minority and female persons are somehow entirely unrelated to those of the dominant culture or cultures (usually white, Anglo-Saxon, Protestant, and male). They ignore these groups' relationship to the development of our current society and imply that the continuous progress of the dominant culture has occurred without any reliance on the contributions and influences of racial and ethnic minorities and women.

6. Linguistic Bias

Language is a powerful conveyer of images in written communications. Use of the generic "he" is an obvious source of bias, but there are also many more subtle forms of linguistic bias. For example some job titles, such as foreman, postman, and fireman, suggest that women cannot perform these jobs. Titles such as supervisor, letter carrier, and fire fighter should be substituted to indicate that the job may be performed by women as well as men.

At some point, we have all had someone misinterpret comments we have made. That is why educators, employers, and parents need to be aware of hidden meanings in their words. Some remarks and words can be interpreted to imply that racial and ethnic groups, women, men, or handicapped persons are superior or inferior to others when the speaker may have no intention of conveying such messages. Word choice may unintentionally distort or shade a message's real meaning.

In a sense, we need to hone word choice to avoid negative or offensive shades of meaning. Such unbiased language plays an important role in encouraging students to explore career options based on their interests, not on prescribed or restricted roles. Unbiased word choice avoids using terms restricted to certain groups or gender.

Following are some brief tips on how to change commonly used gender-biased words.

Word Exchange

Biased	Unbiased
businessman	business manager or executive
chairman	chairperson, leader
cleaning lady	housekeeper, custodian
congressman	member of Congress, congressional representative
craftsman	artisan
craftsmanship	artisanship
fireman	fire fighter
foreman	supervisor, manager
freshman	first-year student
gal Friday	assistant
housewife	homemaker
ladylike	well-mannered
middleman	middle person, intermediary
mailman	letter carrier
man-hour	staff-hour, work hour
mankind	humanity
man-made	synthetic, artificial
manpower	skilled labor, labor force
man-size job	big or enormous job
policeman, policewoman	police officer
repairman	repairer
spokesman	spokesperson, speaker
sportsmanship	sense of fair play
stewardess, steward	flight attendant
workman	worker
workman's compensation	worker's compensation

Sentence Exchange

Biased	Unbiased
The labor force needs skilled men.	The labor force needs skilled men and women.
John Doe is a competent executive, and his wife is a charming blond.	John and Ann make an attractive couple. He's a competent executive, and she's an excellent reporter.
Ask the girls to type the report.	Ask the secretaries to type the report.
She's a career woman.	She's a biologist.
Welcome, ladies and men.	Welcome, ladies and gentlemen. Welcome, women and men.
The executives' wives will assemble.	The executives' spouses will assemble.
A good mechanic knows his customers.	A good mechanic knows his or her customers. Good mechanics know their customers.
It's a pleasure to meet a pretty girl such as you.	It's a pleasure to meet you.
This is Mrs. John Brown.	This is Mrs. Ann Brown. This is Ms. Ann Brown.
John and his wife are homeowners.	John and Ann are homeowners.
Today's young men want opportunities.	Today's young people want opportunities.
Infants need a mother's care.	Infants need parental care.

Biased	Unbiased
She's a tomboy.	She's an energetic and curious person.
He helps his wife at home.	He and his wife share household duties.

Context Exchange

Do you reinforce sex-role stereotypes? For example: the women were calm and rational (implies that most women are emotional and irrational).

Do you quote only men and refer only to notable men of the past or present? Include more references to notable women and minorities.

Do you use descriptions of personality traits that are gender biased? Examples include: her loving attention (careful attention), his brusque manner (blunt manner), and her timid response (hesitant response).

Do you refer to women as being overly concerned with clothing and hairstyle? Men, too, are concerned about their image. Women are also concerned about the economy, the labor force, national affairs, and other universal matters.

Do you refer to men or certain racial or ethnic groups as capable, aggressive, and brave, and to women and other groups of persons as fearful, emotional, and dependent? Men, women and all ethnic and racial groups possess both strengths and weaknesses. Acknowledge all characteristics for all persons.

Between Teacher and Student

"Our teacher, Mr. Greco, was a painter with a poetic soul. Mystical and idiosyncratic in his art, he was real and direct in life. We thrived on this vital contrast. Most teachers warned us to face reality; Mr. Greco endowed us with a sense of mystery. Tragedy and joy were personal acquaintances of his. A refugee, he had known sorrow. Suffering brought him wisdom, which he imparted with grace and nobility (7).

'Stupid idiot!'

'Silly fool!'

'Dumb blockhead!'

Like a rattlesnake, he always had fresh venom. He used to tell us that in his mind he had a picture of a perfect pupil. Compared to this brainchild, we were a dismal disappointment. We were ignorant illiterates wasting professional time and public money. His relentless diatribes undercut our self-respect and ignited our hatred. When he finally fell ill, the whole class celebrated in thanksgiving" (7).

These descriptions show how vividly teachers, for better or worse, are remembered.

Did you ever meet a teacher who changed dry facts into drama and poetry? Can you remember a teacher who belittled you so that you felt incompetent--even worthless? What seem to be the qualities of those teachers who make a positive difference in the lives of their students?

When students are asked to describe successful teachers, one quality that comes up again and again is fairness, the ability to establish a democratic classroom in which all students are treated equally. Although fair and equal treatment of students is important, it is sometimes difficult to achieve. One of the most pervasive barriers is gender bias.

Obviously, teachers would not consciously and intentionally stereotype students. Most teachers work very hard and are extremely conscientious; they try to treat girls and boys in the same way; they want all children to develop to their full potential. However, educators, like members of other professions, have been raised in a society where sexism is prevalent. From parents and counselors, books and television, and myriad societal institutions, teachers have been taught that one set of jobs and behaviors is appropriate for girls and another, different, set is appropriate for boys. However, when teachers are able to recognize the subtle and unintentional gender bias in their behavior, they can make positive changes in their classrooms--and in the lives of their students.

Teacher Expectations: Mind over Matter

It has been said that our thoughts, more specifically our expectations, can have marked effects on the behavior of others. In the classroom, expectations mean the inferences that teachers make about the present and future behavior of their students. In fact, many studies show that when teachers hold certain expectations about their pupils, students actually mold their own behavior to conform to the expectations of their teachers. In schools, the impact of teacher expectations on children has been termed the "self-fulfilling prophecy." Because expectations can be so important, a closer look at this phenomenon is needed. Consider the following example:

The children in an elementary school in a lower-class neighborhood were administered a special test designed to identify students who were "intellectual bloomers" and who would most likely show remarkable academic gains during the coming school year. About 20 percent of the students were identified by the test as "intellectual bloomers," and their teachers were informed of the test results. The validity of the test was demonstrated eight months later when these intellectual bloomers were given an I.Q. test and scored higher than they had on previous I.Q. examinations. Apparently the new test could be hailed an important breakthrough, for it could effectively identify which students would demonstrate unusual I.Q. gains. Or could it?

And now, the test of the example....

The test given was not a predictor of intellectual bloomers at all. It was a standard intelligence test, and students were not identified in any way through their test scores. In fact, the 20 percent were not really intellectual bloomers. Their names were selected at random. Yet, their I.Q. scores did increase while the scores of the rest of the students remained stable.

According to Robert Rosenthal and Lenore Jacobson, who conducted this study, the key here was teacher expectations. Because teachers thought that these children would be intellectual bloomers, they behaved in various subtle ways to promote and encourage this development; in short, teacher expectations shaped and altered student academic performance. Further, by the end of the study, teachers described these randomly selected students as happier, more curious, more interesting, and more likely to succeed in later life than other children. This study was reported in a book entitled Pygmalion in the Classroom, and it is a well-known example of the "self-fulfilling prophecy"(17).

When this study was first released, it generated a great deal of interest not only among teachers and parents but among educational researchers as well. Study after study was conducted to determine if teacher expectations could really affect student behavior and achievement. Some studies have confirmed that teacher expectations can affect student behavior. Some have not. Even though conflicting evidence remains in the wake of the original Pygmalion in the Classroom study, many researchers conclude that teacher expectations can influence student behavior. Following is a little more background on how this process works.

1. Early in the school year, teachers form expectations about what students can achieve and how they will behave.

Some of these expectations may be inaccurate and difficult to change.

2. Based on these expectations, teachers treat students differently. When these expectations are inaccurate and rigid, treatment of students will be inappropriate.
3. Sometimes, students will actually change their own behavior so that it conforms to teacher expectations. Two researchers, Jere Brophy and Thomas Good, summarize this process. "If continued indefinitely, such treatment constitutes a pressure on the student to begin to conform to the teacher's expectations by behaving in the ways that the teacher expects the student to behave. This in turn reinforces the teacher's expectations all the more, and a self-regenerating vicious circle is established. If the situation persists, a true expectation effect is likely to occur"(1).

Living Up--and Down--to Sex-Stereotyped Expectations

As teachers enter the classroom, they carry with them more than their dittos and chalk; they also carry socially influenced beliefs about what are appropriate behaviors, values, and careers for girls and for boys. Many teachers, like other members of society, have been socialized to believe that girls should be passive, demure, sweet, and dependent; they think that boys should be assertive, athletic, and competitive. For example, a group of junior high school teachers was asked to describe good female and good male students. Their responses are given in Table 3 (12).

What happens to students who do not fit the stereotypes? The athletic girl who is super in math, assertive in her interpersonal style, and hopeful of becoming a corporate president may receive a variety of negative messages. The boy who likes poetry and ballet, or who expresses the hope of becoming a secretary or nurse or kindergarten teacher will also be treated to negative signals. Such messages confine students, limit their options, and restrict their aspirations and potential.

One researcher conducted in-depth interviews in which she asked women to remember their school days and what it was like to grow up female. Their recollections show that they were very aware of sex-stereotyped teacher expectations. "We always expected the boys to be doing funny things, like putting pencils in the heater, or putting the teacher's chair outside or yelling in the class--all those kinds of things. And I always felt that when I did the same things that I thought were funny and were neat to be in on, that I got scolded in a way that they never did" (13).

When men think back over their experiences in school, they also talk about the pressures and the pain of conforming to sex-role stereotypes--especially in athletics. The two best players (never me) were captains, and they chose--one by one--players for their teams. The choosing went on and on, the better players getting picked first and me and my type last. During the game, I always played outfield. Right field. Far right field. And there I would stand in the hot sun wishing I was anywhere else in the world" (15).

Sex-stereotyped expectations can also have a harmful impact on boys in academic areas. For example, research shows that when teachers expect boys to do as well as girls in beginning reading, male students live up to these expectations. However, when teachers do not expect boys to perform as well as girls in beginning reading, they actually fail to match the performance of their female classmates (14).

For girls an expectation problem is more likely to occur in math and science. Math has been stereotyped a male domain and girls receive the message (23). While girls' performance in math is equal to that of boys at age nine, their performance continues to drop as they "progress" through school (16). These young women learn to perceive math as inconsequential to future careers, and they are far less likely to take advanced math courses than are boys. By young adulthood, the gap between male and female achievement scores in math can only be described as staggering. Further, math acts as a "critical filter" that denies women access to a whole range of scientific and technical occupations.

Most teachers care deeply about the students in their classrooms. When asked if they treat boys and girls differently, they are usually startled. "Of course not," they reply. "I treat all my students, girls and boys, in the same manner." However, when teachers are encouraged to analyze their attitudes and behaviors, they discover the subtle and pervasive nature of sex bias in the classroom; they become concerned, and they make changes. In fact, teachers, because of the special relationship they have with their students, can help counteract the limiting cycle of sex bias.

Teachers Talk, but Not in the Same Way to Everyone

The noted educator, Haim Ginott, used to tell a story about the little girl who came home from her first day of school. "How did you like it?" her anxious mother queried. "Oh, school was just fine," the young scholar replied, "except for this one lady who kept interrupting."

On one level this anecdote captures the funny notions young children have about what school is supposed to be like. On another level this story shows how insightful young children can be about classroom rituals and norms. This girl accurately picked up one of the patterns that is likely to characterize not only the first day of school, but every day thereafter. Teachers do a great deal of interrupting.

In fact, they do a great deal of talking in general. For example, Ned Flanders, one of the earliest and best-known researchers in classroom-interaction analysis, determined that approximately two-thirds of classroom talk is teacher talk (5). Another researcher, Phil Jackson, noted that teachers typically engage in over one thousand verbal exchanges in their classrooms every day (9). And another researcher tells us that teachers typically ask between three and six questions every minute (6), and after asking a question, they are likely to wait only one second for a student to answer (18). If this instantaneous response is not forthcoming, they will call on someone else, answer the question themselves, or ask a new question. If the impression you are getting from studies like these is that teachers do a great deal of fast talking, you are right.

Given the hectic pace of classroom life, it is no wonder teachers have little time to think about the subtleties and specifics of verbal interaction. They are amazed to discover the rapid-fire rate at which they ask questions. They are also surprised to learn that they do not interact with female students in the same way that they do with males. The only sex difference in verbal interaction that teachers typically are aware of is in classroom discipline. "Yes, I suppose I reprimand boys more and punish them more," many teachers will agree. "But the boys seem to be the ones who are misbehaving."

Educators who are concerned about equality of opportunity in schools have been examining life in classrooms. Who do teachers talk to? Praise? Reprimand? Question? Do certain students fail to receive their fair share of the teacher's verbal attention, not only in terms of quantity but in quality as well? Are minority students and female students the "invisible" members of our classrooms, ignored when questions are asked and passed over when teacher praise, encouragement, and reward are passed out? And researchers are trying to determine if the way teachers interact with students makes a difference. Does the quantity and quality of teacher interaction appear to have any impact on student self-concept, behavior, and achievement?

Following are some classroom scenarios. As you read each story, try to determine if there are differences in the ways the teachers treat male and female students. Each scenario is followed by a review of the research on which it is based. If the vignettes appear to be somewhat exaggerated, it is because they are illustrations designed to reflect information drawn from several research studies.

Teachers Talk with Boys and Girls: A Play-by-Play Research Review

The Play

It is a hot Friday afternoon in June a few days before summer vacation. Jim Bernstein's loosened tie hangs askew around his neck, his wilted jacket has been tossed across a pile of ungraded papers, and his shirt is pasted to his back. It has been one of those difficult days with the sixth graders, and his patience is thin.

"O.K. class. Cut the noise. You boys in the back row. I think I've made it clear that the assignment is in-class reading, not in-class talking. This is your last chance." Despite this warning, the back-row clamor continues unabated.

"That does it! Jim, Pete, Mark! Put your names on the board! Stop stalling--you know where. Right there on the after-school list. It's a half-hour detention tonight...maybe longer if you don't watch out. Now, unless the rest of you want to join this unholy trio, you'll get back to your reading assignment." The class grows momentarily still except for the shuffling of books and the turning of pages. But the lull is short-lived, and Mr. Bernstein turns disciplinarian again.

"Alan and Susan. This is not a place for your own private gabfest. You know the penalty. Alan, your name goes on the after-school list. Put it up there right now. And Susan," Mr. Bernstein's voice softens, "I'm surprised to have to talk to you like this. You know better. One more chance, and then your name goes up on the list and you'll join the boys after school."

Before you read ahead, take a few moments to summarize the interaction patterns in Mr. Bernstein's classroom.

The Research

Did you notice that Mr. Bernstein spent most of his time reprimanding the boys in his classroom? How typical is this interaction pattern? Do boys in classrooms usually get reprimanded more often than girls? Are boys really that much more disruptive?

Researchers have looked at how teachers dispense disapproval: in study after study, they find that boys get most of it. Moreover, most of the disapproval that male students receive is directed at classroom behavior. One study indicates that boys receive eight to ten times as many prohibitory control messages as their female classmates(10)--Stop talking, Bob; Put that comic book away, Bill; Back to your seat, Andrew.

At this point you may be wondering why boys are disciplined more frequently. A logical and simple answer is that boys tend to misbehave more, and classroom observation studies support this conclusion. However, this is only a partial explanation.

One study of fifteen preschool classes showed that when teachers were faced with disruptive behavior, from both boys and girls, they were over three times more likely to reprimand the boys than the girls. Further, they more frequently punished the boys with a loud public reprimand. In contrast, when they did reprimand girls, they were likely to do it quickly and quietly (22). Therefore, even when both girls and boys are misbehaving, boys receive more frequent and more harsh discipline.

The difference in intensity as well as in quantity of disapproval emerges as a finding in several studies. In addition to getting more than their share of disapproving messages, boys are scolded more loudly and more harshly than girls, even when the offenses are similar or identical. In the preceding vignette, did you notice that Susan received a softer rebuke than her classmate Alan? Also, she was not given the same punishment that Alan was, even though she was involved in identical classroom misbehavior.

It is important to realize that all boys do not receive these disapproving messages. It is the low-achieving boys who attract most of this negative attention. For example, one study showed that, while low-achieving boys raised their hands to respond less than half as often as their classmates, they were criticized more than twice as frequently (1).

The research indicates that Mr. Bernstein is quite representative in the way he reprimands boys and girls. There was no information in this vignette about the socioeconomic or racial backgrounds of his students. If there had been, and if Mr. Bernstein remained representative, you might have found him disciplining minority students and children from lower socioeconomic groups more frequently (1). This is another pattern that emerges from the educational research on classroom interaction.

The Play

It looked as though a cyclone had swept through Ms. Washington's classroom. In fact, it was a cyclone of a human sort--final rehearsal of the eighth-grade play. The students were getting ready to put on Light in the Forest, the story of an American Indian boy caught between two cultures. Despite the chaos of last-minute rehearsal, Gloria Washington was clearly a teacher in charge of the situation. She moved smoothly from one knot of students to another, offering advice on costumes, scenery, sound effects, and script.

"John, that tepee of yours seems to be a little shaky. I doubt it will make it through the first act, let alone the whole play. Why don't you fasten the poles together more tightly at the top? Go get the box of rope from the resource room. That should make it strong enough."

"Maria, how are those headbands coming along? They seem to be shedding feathers. Here, give them to me and I'll show you how to fasten the feathers more firmly. Just let me add a little glue, and you'll find your problem is solved."

"Laura and Ann, you look like you're having trouble measuring the canvas to fit over that drum. Give me the tape measure for a second. There, I've marked it off. I think that will fit."

"Brian and Tony. That background mural really looks great. Just add a little more orange to the sunset, and you're finished."

"Mike, let me hear the background music you have on the tape recorder. That sounds good. It does a nice job setting the mood for the play."

"What's the matter, Joseph? Part of the script giving you trouble? The dialogue in Scene II just doesn't sound right, does it? Here's what I suggest. Reread the first chapter in Light in the Forest and that will give you a better idea of how True Son's mind works and how he would be likely to talk and behave."

"Dennis, let's take a look at the opening narration you're working on. Hmmm, this does a pretty good job, but as you revise it, I want you to think about these questions: How much background information will the audience need to understand the first scene? What words could you use that will get the audience's attention and give them a feeling for the problem that True Son faces?"

Because this scene is fairly complex, you'll notice that we focused on teacher comments, and we did not include student responses. Before you read ahead, think about the comments Ms. Washington made. Were there any sex differences in the way she talked to and worked with her students?

The Research

In the last scene, the teacher did not spend her time reprimanding; nevertheless, did you notice that the boys still received more of her attention? In fact, teachers not only disapprove of boys more, but they also interact with them more in general. While the research is not entirely consistent on the nature of this interaction, certain patterns emerge.

Teachers appear to interact more with boys in four major categories: disapproval, praise and approval, instruction, and listening to the child (25).

They initiate more work contacts, more academic contacts, and more positive contacts with boys (11). Teachers are also more likely to engage in extended conversations with male students (21).

Teachers ask boys more direct questions, more open-ended questions (11), more complex and abstract questions (24).

When working with gifted students, teachers favor boys and are more restrictive with girls (2).

Teachers are more likely to give male students extended directions, detailed instructions on how to do things for themselves. In contrast, they are less likely to explain things to girls. Teachers tend to do things for the girls instead. Here is a specific example of how this happens in the classroom.

In one classroom, the children were making party baskets. When the time came to staple the paper handles...[the teacher] showed the boys how to use the stapler by holding the handle in place while the child stapled it. On the girls' turns, however, if the child didn't spontaneously staple the handle herself, the teacher took the basket [and] stapled it (21).

These studies show that boys are the prominent members of classrooms and receive more of the teachers' positive and active attention. In contrast, girls are more frequently passed over and ignored. Were you able to analyze the classroom scene above to determine some of these patterns? Did you notice that the boys received more academic contacts, more questions and more approval? Also, did you notice that when male students were having difficulty, Ms. Washington gave them directions on how to solve the problem for themselves? But when girls needed help, Ms. Washington took over and did it for them instead of instructing them on how to do it for themselves.

It is important to qualify the research we have presented. Not all boys are receiving this positive and active attention. Low-achieving boys receive more teacher criticism, in contrast, high-achieving boys receive more teacher approval and active instruction. The difference is so clear that some researchers have concluded that "In many ways, in so far as teacher-student interaction data are concerned, it makes sense to speak of low-achieving boys and high-achieving boys as separate groups rather than to speak of boys as a single group" (1).

Boys, especially high-achieving boys, receive approval, questions, detailed instructions, and, in general, more active teaching attention. Girls of all ability-levels do not interact as frequently with teachers. Nor do students who are members of minority groups. For example, one study shows that teachers give less attention to black students; they request fewer statements from blacks, encourage them to expand on ideas less frequently, praise them less, and criticize them more (19). Other studies show similar patterns of invisibility for Mexican-American and native American children (1).

The Play

It is a few minutes before third period, and the students in Ms. Watson's seventh-grade English class are anxious.

"Do you think she's got the tests graded?"

"That test was so long. I don't know if she's had the time."

"You know Watson. She always gets tests back the next day. She's famous for it."

"I'm scared. She said this test would be half our grade. Do you think she means it?"

Eyes turn to the front of the room as Ms. Watson enters and places her briefcase on the desk. She pulls out a pile of papers decorated with red-pencil marks, and the class grows quiet.

"As you know, students, yesterday you took a very important English exam. It covered a lot of information--everything that we've been discussing for the last four weeks in our unit on poetry. We'll use this class period for individual conferences on the test. I'm going to call each of you up to my desk so we can discuss this test in some detail. I want to make sure that you understand why you got the grade you did and what areas you need to work on."

"While I'm having these individual conferences, I'd like the rest of you to be working on your assignment in the language-skills book. Tom Johnson, come up to my desk, please."

"Here's your exam, Tom. Take a few minutes to look it over, and then we'll discuss it."

The students glance from their assignment to see Tom's reaction. They watch as he skims through the test and then smiles.

"What's your reaction to the grade, Tom?"

"I'm really happy. I thought I'd done O.K., but I wasn't sure."

"You did a very fine job on this exam. An A- is something to be proud of. You identified all the spot passages accurately and you gave correct definitions for the figures of speech. I particularly like the original poem you wrote in the extra-credit section of the exam, and I wrote a long comment about it that you can read more carefully at your seat."

"On the negative side, I must say something about the appearance of this exam. Maybe you were nervous while you were taking the test, but that still doesn't excuse this kind of careless writing. The prescriptions my doctor writes out are easier to read than this. And you know the rules about margins, headings, and the proper form for all work that gets handed in. Work on getting things in proper shape and in the next test maybe you can turn an A- into a straight A. Next, Beth Galente."

Beth reluctantly accepts the paper Ms. Watson hands her.

"Take a few minutes to read the test over, Beth, and then we'll talk about it."

"A C+! I thought I had done better than that."

"Well, you confused the definitions of metaphor and simile, and you left out personification. Also, you seem to have irony mixed up with alliteration."

"I didn't realize I missed so many of the questions."

"Why don't you look your paper over more carefully at your desk to make sure you understand the errors. Next, Frank Campone."

Frank slumps down in the chair next to Ms. Watson's desk and looks despondent as he goes over the test.

"Do you have any questions about the exam, Frank?"

"I don't know if I have questions, but my parents sure will. They're gonna kill me. They expect me to get A's and B's."

"Well, they're right, Frank, you should be getting A's and B's. But you can't just walk in and take the exam without studying. Also, you have to pay more attention during class. Passing notes to your buddies and doing social studies homework behind your poetry books isn't going to get you those A's and B's that both you and your parents want. Neither will turning in hastily scrawled work--obviously done at the last minute--that I can hardly read. Now, I know you can do better than this, but you have to give it more effort."

As Frank returns to his seat, Ms. Watson calls Marilyn Miller to her desk.

"Here Marilyn, look over your paper and then we'll discuss your grade." Marilyn spends a few minutes intently going over the questions.

"What's your reaction?"

"Well, a B+ is a pretty good grade, but I wish I could have gotten an A on this test....I knew I couldn't remember a few of those spot passages, so I just guessed. I guess I guessed wrong."

"I know you would have liked a higher grade. You're very well behaved in class--you seem to be paying attention, your papers are always handed in on time, and your work is neat and careful. However, you did miss some of the questions. You should check over the spot-passage section. You identified several of these incorrectly. Also go over your explanation of the Robert Frost poem. I don't think you understand how complex this poem is."

What teacher-student interaction patterns characterize this classroom? Do you notice any differences in the way Ms. Watson evaluates the work of her male and female students? Summarize these patterns in your mind before you read ahead.

The Research

As discussed, there are a number of studies showing that, in general, boys are disciplined more frequently and more harshly in schools, and that they receive more extended conversation and direct instructions, and more praise than girls. In contrast, girls receive less attention and are more likely to be the "invisible" members of our classrooms than boys are.

To date, there have been fewer studies exploring subtleties in the different ways teachers talk to boys and girls about their academic work. While the educational literature is not conclusive in this area, the studies that have been done must be looked at carefully because they have important implications for teachers. Recent studies by Carol Dweck and her colleagues provide more fine-grained analyses of the kinds of criticism that girls and boys receive in classrooms. These studies make a persuasive case that there are striking sex differences in the amount and kind of praise and criticism students receive for their academic work.

Researchers observed fourth- and fifth-grade classrooms over a period of five weeks. The observers coded and analyzed the evaluative feedback that teachers gave to girls and boys. These researchers found that approximately 90 percent of the praise boys received for their academic work was directly concerned with intellectual quality (e.g., John, you did a good job analyzing the causes of the Civil War). In contrast, for girls only 80 percent of praise for academic work was directly concerned with intellectual quality. The other 20 percent of the praise that girls received for their work did not focus on intellectual quality. Instead this praise was directed at papers being neat, pretty, and following the rules of form (e.g., That's a nice paper, Suzy. Your margins and headings are exactly right) (3).

In the classroom scene above, did you notice the different ways Ms. Watson handled the male student and the female student who did well on the exam? Tom was praised for the intellectual quality of his answers. Marilyn was praised for promptly handing in neat papers.

Studies also indicate that in terms of criticism for academic work the sex differences are even more striking. Approximately one-half the criticism boys receive on their academic work is for intellectual inadequacy. The other half of the criticism boys get is for failure to obey the rules of form and failure to turn in papers that are neat and attractive. In contrast, almost 90 percent of the criticism girls receive for academic work is specifically directed at intellectual inadequacy. Girls get little criticism on neatness and rules of form (4).

Did you notice the different kinds of criticism for academic work that Ms. Watson gave to boys and girls? Both A- student Tom and C- student Frank were criticized for handing in sloppy work that violated rules about margins, headings, and the like. The two girls did not receive this kind of disapproval. Instead both C+ student Beth and B+ student Marilyn received criticism that focused directly on the intellectual inadequacy of their exam responses.

Researchers who analyze differences in the ways teachers criticize the academic work of girls and boys have discovered another very important pattern. When teachers criticize boys, they tend to attribute their academic inadequacies to lack of effort (4). (You defined these terms incorrectly, Bill. I know you can do better if you try harder.) However, when teachers criticize girls, they usually do not attribute intellectual inadequacy to lack of effort (You defined these terms incorrectly, Alice). In the preceding classroom scene, did you notice that Ms. Watson attributed Frank's C- to a lack of effort and encouraged him to try harder? In contrast, no such attribution to effort was made for Beth's C+. Table 2 summarizes the research on how teachers evaluate the academic work of boys and girls.

Table 2
Teacher Evaluation for Academic Work of Boys and Girls
(in percentage)

Item	Boys	Girls
Praise		
Intellectual quality	90	80
Following the rules of form	10	20
Criticism		
Intellectual inadequacy	50	90
Failure to obey the rules of form and other nonintellectual factors	50	10
Attribution to effort (you can do better if you try)	frequent	infrequent

Impact and Implications

This play-by-play research has presented information about the differences in the ways teachers interact with girls and boys in their classrooms. It is important to mention that it does not seem to make a difference whether it is a man or a woman who stands behind the teacher's desk. The interaction patterns we have discussed remain virtually the same (1).

If you have been thinking like a researcher, you are probably already considering the next question. Does it matter if teachers interact differently with girls and boys? Do these differences in any way affect student learning and behavior?

This seems to be a fairly straightforward question. Paradoxically, the answer is somewhat roundabout and complex. It is difficult to make direct cause-and-effect links between teacher behavior and pupil attitudes and achievement. Therefore, we cannot make definitive statements about how teacher interaction affects student behavior. However, we can look very carefully at what educational researchers and theorists tell us and draw some conclusions.

One researcher, Pauline Sears, studied classroom-interaction patterns over fifteen years ago, long before the concept of sex equity emerged on our educational consciousness. She concluded that "One consequence might be a cumulative increase in independent, autonomous behavior by boys as they are disapproved, praised, listened to, and taught more actively by the teacher. Another might be a lowering of self-esteem generally for girls as they receive less attention and are criticized for their lack of knowledge and skill" (20).

Her words set the scene for contemporary educational research and practice. In fact, the studies of Carol Dweck and her colleagues indicate that this indeed is the result.

Dweck has found that there are sex differences in a pattern of behavior called "learned helplessness." Learned helplessness exists when failure is perceived as insurmountable. Children who exhibit learned helplessness attribute failure to factors that they cannot control, for example, lack of ability. After receiving negative evaluation, children characterized by learned helplessness are likely to show further deterioration in performance. In contrast, children who have had factors emphasized that can be modified or changed, such as effort, tend to see failure as surmountable. After negative evaluation, these children will often show improved performance.

Girls are more likely than boys to exhibit learned helplessness. They are more likely to blame poor performance on lack of ability rather than on lack of effort. They are also "more prone than boys to show decreased persistence or impaired performance following failure, the threat of failure or increased evaluative pressure" (4).

Why are girls so ready to give up after receiving failure feedback? Why do boys exhibit greater confidence in their abilities and show greater persistence in failure situations?

At least part of the answer can be found in the way teachers talk to students about their academic work. As we have discussed, teachers give boys more general and intellectually irrelevant disapproval. They criticize them for misbehavior, for not following directions, for violating the rules of form. They give less criticism to boys for the intellectual quality of their academic work. When they do criticize boys for intellectual inadequacy, they frequently attribute failure to lack of effort. As a result of such frequent and diffuse negative feedback, boys are more likely to attribute failure, not to themselves, but to a generally negative attitude on the part of the teacher or to the fact that they have not expended sufficient effort.

For girls, the pattern is different. Girls do not receive frequent, general, and intellectually irrelevant disapproval. They are not often criticized for misbehavior or for failing to comply with the rules of form. Almost all of the criticism girls receive is related directly and specifically to intellectual inadequacy. Moreover, this feedback is not usually tempered by the comment, You could have done better. You just didn't try hard enough. As a result, girls are left with few options for placing blame. They cannot attribute failure to a teacher who is "against" them or to a lack of effort. The cause of failure must then lie in their own lack of ability. In short, Dweck hypothesized that teachers' evaluative feedback regarding the intellectual quality of academic work may actually cause sex differences in learned helplessness.

To test this hypothesis, Dweck and her colleagues conducted an interesting experiment with sixty fifth-grade children. Ten boys and ten girls were randomly assigned to each of three experimental conditions. In one experimental condition, ten boys and ten girls were taken individually to a testing room where they were presented with word puzzles. The children were given two kinds of failure feedback for their performance. One kind of feedback was specifically addressed to the correctness of the solution (e.g., You didn't do very well that time--you didn't get the word right). The other kind of failure feedback was explicitly addressed to a nonintellectual aspect of performance (e.g., You didn't do very well that time--it wasn't neat enough). This was called the "teacher-boy condition" because it is similar to the kind of negative evaluation that boys are more likely to receive in classrooms. Each of the other two experimental conditions consisted of ten boys and ten girls. In these conditions the children also worked individually in a testing room on word puzzles. However, the failure feedback these children received was addressed specifically to the correctness of the solution. These children did not receive failure feedback addressed to a nonintellectual aspect of their performance, such as neatness. These were called the "teacher-girl conditions" because they approximated the kind of negative evaluation girls are more likely to receive in classrooms.

At the end of the word-puzzle trials, the children in all three conditions were given written questions that assessed whether they attributed failure to the instructors' unfairness, to their own lack of effort, or to their own lack of ability. Most of the children in the "teacher-boy condition" did not view failure on the word puzzles as reflecting a lack of ability. Both boys and girls in this condition indicated that insufficient effort was the cause of failure. In sharp contrast, both girls and boys in the two "teacher-girl conditions" overwhelmingly interpreted the failure feedback as indicating a lack of ability. This research led the experimenters to conclude that "the pattern of evaluative feedback given to boys and girls in the classroom can result directly in girls' greater tendency to view failure feedback as indicative of their level of ability" (4). Therefore, the way teachers interact with children can have important consequences--an impact that can cause a sex difference in the appearance of learned helplessness. Girls see failure as insurmountable because it appears to be caused by their own lack of ability.

Another potential impact results from the greater amount of active instruction that boys receive, not only praise and disapproval, but also questions, opportunities for recitation, extended conversations and directions. This active instruction may not only increase "independent autonomous behavior" in boys, as Pauline Sears noted, and increase confidence in ability and persistence in the face of failure, as Carol Dweck noted, it may also influence sex differences in achievement.

Recent research on teacher effectiveness indicates that a pattern of teaching behavior called "direct instruction" appears to be very important in increasing student achievement. Direct instruction involves active teaching; it includes the setting goals, assessing student progress, making active and clear presentations of the concepts under study; giving clear instruction for class and individual work (8). The interaction research we have discussed indicates that teachers appear to be instructing boys more actively and directly than girls. And, as presented in the first two readings, "Gender Bias in Schools," and "Sexism in Education," there are clear sex differences in patterns of achievement.

What happens to girls after the middle-elementary years that puts an end to their promising academic start? Obviously, many factors must be considered. And one of these factors may be the less active and direct teaching that female students receive in our nation's classrooms.

Teachers can make a difference in the lives of their students. If you are to have a positive impact on the achievement of all your students, it is essential that you not only become aware of biases in teacher-student interaction patterns, but that you consciously, intentionally, and affirmatively develop interaction skills that are fair, equitable, and designed to actively compensate for student differences in behavior and achievement.

Putting Your Knowledge to Work

The rapid pace of classroom life makes careful observation a challenge; however, by keeping some general principles in mind and using the observation instruments provided, you can acquire a number of helpful insights into your teaching behavior. A basic step is to collect objective information about your teaching. You can do this on your own in a number of ways. You can set up a video or audio recorder in your classroom to record your teaching. Or, you can cooperate with another teacher and take turns observing each other's work. A point to remember is that the demands on you as a teacher are far too great for you to try to maintain an ongoing and objective analysis of your own behavior. Therefore, you must begin by identifying a source to help you collect information about your teaching.

The following suggested observation techniques run the gamut from the simple to the complex. You may want to start slowly with some of the initial techniques, and, as you become more comfortable with the observation process, move on to the more complex approaches. Obviously, the more information you acquire, the better you will be able to pinpoint and alter potentially biased teaching patterns.

To get the best results, use each technique for about thirty minutes, and, if possible, use each several times. This will provide the most representative sample of your teaching behaviors.

Observation Technique 1: Teacher Attention

To determine whether you are giving approximately equal attention to boys and girls, ask an observer to count the number of times you interact with each. Or, if you have an audio or video recorder set up, you may be able to assess your own interaction style. For this initial technique, all of your comments are counted, including questions, answers, rewards, directions, and so forth to either a girl or a boy. Only when you speak to the entire class or to a mixed group of girls and boys are the comments not counted.

Because any given class might have an imbalanced sex ratio, you can get an accurate proportion by dividing each total by the number of boys and girls in the room. An example follows.

Boys 48 (total number of teacher interactions)
13 (total number of boys in the class) = 3.7 average interactions with each boy

Girls 22 (total number of teacher interactions)
12 (total number of girls in the class) = 1.8 average interactions with each girl

Finding: The teacher gives boys more than twice as many interactions as girls.

Obviously, this is a comparable indicator of who is receiving your attention. If you want more specific information, you may want to divide the tallies into academic and nonacademic attention, and see how attention to boys and girls is distributed in these two areas. Academic attention would involve questions, rewards, and other comments directed at the student's work. Nonacademic comments would include disciplining students, class routine and decorum, and other remarks not concerned with a student's academic work.

When you use this observation system to observe other teachers, or when this approach is used to analyze your own teaching, you will be able to compare these results with the research findings that indicate that most of the teacher's attention, academic and nonacademic, is given to boys. Do your teaching behaviors reflect this pattern, or do you distribute attention in a fair manner to both female and male students?

Observation Technique 2: Praise and Criticism

To obtain more specific information, you can use the same procedure described in the first technique, but this time distinguish between teacher interactions that praise students and those that criticize students. So for the comment, Good answer, Betty, tally one mark for girls in the reward category. A comment such as, Pay attention, Joan, would be recorded by a tally for girls in the criticism category. The remark, Don, see me after class about your poor behavior, would receive a tally in the boys' criticism column. A comment such as, Good work, Jim, would be noted in the boys' reward column. As in the first procedure, you then divide each tally by the total number of boys and the total number of girls to get the average. This procedure will allow you to compare how frequently you reward boys versus girls, and how frequently you reprimand one sex compared to the other.

The average boy has a 60 percent chance of being reprimanded. The average girl stands only an 8 percent chance of being reprimanded. Boys are being reprimanded six times more often than girls.

As with the first procedure, you may want to get more specific information about praise and criticism. To do this, divide the tallies between praise and criticism that are related to academic attention of the teacher.

Observation Technique 3: Teacher Questions

Your use of questions represents another area that can reflect either sex bias or sex equity. How do you distribute your questions among boys and girls?

Using the same procedure described in Observation Techniques 1 and 2, tally the distribution of questions given to girls and boys. Divide these tallies by the number of girls present and the number of boys present to determine the average number of questions a typical boy and a typical girl would receive. Compare these averages to see if you are practicing equity or promoting bias.

Observation Technique 4: Assessment of Sex Equity in Teacher Interactions

This observation technique is far more comprehensive than the first three techniques. In fact, this procedure subsumes those three techniques and goes beyond them to analyze a wide variety of teacher behaviors. If you have had previous experience in recording and analyzing teacher behaviors, you may want to bypass the first three techniques and begin with this one.

Although this technique uses the same basic procedure as the previous techniques, tallying teacher behaviors, this observation technique investigates a wider spectrum of teacher behaviors, and you will be kept busy counting them all. However, you will be rewarded for this effort by obtaining a fairly comprehensive picture of your teaching in relation to sex equity.

Begin by looking over the observation sheet (see page 150) and reviewing the following definitions of each of the categories.

Observation Categories

I. Praise
   A. Academic. Rewards and reinforcement given for the intellectual quality of work: Good answer. You've written a very interesting report. Your evaluation of the problem is excellent.

B. Nonacademic. All rewards and reinforcements not directed to the intellectual quality of academic work: You're being nice and quiet today. That's an attractive dress. That's a very neatly written paper.

II. Academic Criticism

A. Intellectual quality. Critical remarks directed at the lack of intellectual quality of work: Perhaps math isn't a good field for you. Is this experiment too difficult for you? You don't seem able to grasp this material.

B. Effort. Comments attributing academic failure to lack of effort: You're not trying hard enough. I know you can do the work if you put your mind to it and study harder.

III. Nonacademic Criticism

A. Mild. Negative comments that reprimand violations of conduct, rules, forms, behavior, and other nonacademic areas: Tom, stay in line. Sally, quiet down. Jim, your paper is too messy.

B. Harsh. These negative comments make scenes and attract attention. They are louder, often longer, and always stronger than mild criticism: Tom, get back in line; I've had more than enough from you today; stay in line or suffer the consequences; move. Harriet, the rules are quite straightforward, and you are talking again and disturbing others, for violating the rules, you are to stay after class today for one hour in the detention hall.

IV. Questions

A. Low-level. Questions that require memory on the part of the student: When did Columbus arrive in the Americas? Who was the fifth president? What is the name of this color?

B. High-level. Questions that require higher intellectual processes and ask the student to use information, not just memorize it: In your opinion, why did Columbus come to America? Analyze the causes of the Vietnam War. Determine the range of possible answers in this quadratic equation. How would you evaluate this painting? Can you apply the rules of supply and demand to the following example? How would you write your own personal statement on human rights?

V. Academic Intervention

A. Facilitative. Behaviors that facilitate learning by providing students with suggestions, hints, and cues to encourage and enable them to complete the task for themselves. The teacher helps, but the student does the work: Think of yesterday's formula, and try to do that problem again. Double check your facts. Your explanation isn't complete; review the purpose of the law, and then try it again. Watch me do this experiment, then you try it again by yourself.

B. Disruptive. Comments that prevent or short-circuit success because the teacher intrudes and takes over the process. The teacher does the task for the student. When the teacher provides the answer instead of the direction, this category is tallied: Let me do that for you. That's wrong--the answer is 14. You're way off base; watch me do it.

An analysis of your findings can be made by averaging the tallies and comparing the average results for girls with the average for boys. As you assess your results, see if you are practicing equitable teaching behavior. Consider the following guidelines and potential problems as you evaluate your teaching.

<u>Praise</u>. Are boys and girls receiving approximately the same amount of praise? Are boys and girls receiving praise for academic and nonacademic efforts in about the same proportion? Or, are boys more likely to receive praise for the intellectual quality of their work?

<u>Academic Criticism</u>. Are equal amounts of academic criticism given to girls and boys? Or, are boys admonished for not trying hard enough while girls are criticized for lack of ability and competence?

<u>Nonacademic Criticism</u>. Are boys and girls receiving the same amounts of criticism at the same level? Or, are boys receiving more frequent and harsher criticism for classroom misbehavior?

Questions. Are the number and types of questions asked divided equally? Or, are boys asked more questions, particularly higher-level questions?

Academic Intervention. Is the learning of girls and boys facilitated or encouraged? Or, are boys shown how to solve problems and accomplish tasks, while girls have these activities done for them?

Observation Technique 5: Descriptive Data

The first four observation techniques rely on counting certain types of teacher behaviors. However, to uncover additional information, which will offer you specific examples of your classroom interaction style, record objective descriptions, verbatim if possible, of the classroom activity being analyzed.

For example, select the first category on the previous observation sheet, praise. To develop a more in-depth understanding of the use of praise in the classroom an observer would record precisely all statements of praise and reward. If you are using an audio or video recorder, you would play it back after class and write down these comments yourself. This procedure provides precise information about the kinds of praise being used for boys and girls. Here's an example:

Praise Given Boys	Praise Given Girls
Excellent answer, Miguel.	Good, Shari.
Right, Bill.	That's a beautiful cover for your project, Myra.
Good thinking, Joe.	O.K., good answer, Consuela.
Fine response, Tony.	That's a neatly written paper, Chantal.
That's a great idea, David.	Jane, that's the right idea.
I really like that solution, Tom.	
That's right on target, Tulsi.	
Excellent, Joe.	

From this kind of descriptive information, you can discover several aspects of teacher behavior. The teacher is giving more praise to boys than to girls, and more of this praise is directed at academic achievement. Also, the teacher is praising girls for neatness and attractiveness of work as well as for intellectual accomplishments.

As you can see from this brief example, obtaining descriptive data provides you with more information than simply tallying the behaviors. This process can be applied to the other categories as well; record your questions, criticisms, and the like. Although this technique is somewhat more demanding than the previous three, it has potential for providing you with some very specific and valuable information.

Another technique for obtaining more precise information is to tally not the number of teacher comments in a particular category, but the amount of time a teacher gives to that category. For example, a teacher may ask only one question, but that question could require three seconds of classroom time, or it might require thirty seconds of classroom time. A more precise observation procedure would take into consideration these differences in time. After all, the more time a teacher spends in a category, the more important that category becomes in its impact on students.

Those of you familiar with the well-known Flanders Interaction Analysis system will already know about the procedures for measuring how much time a teacher spends in each category. Some observers rely on stopwatches, others can mentally count with remarkable accuracy the time spent by the teacher in each category. If you have had experience using the Flanders or a similar procedure, apply that knowledge to one or more of the observation techniques described in this unit. This will obviously give you a more precise indication of patterns of gender bias or equity in the classroom.

If, on the other hand, you have not had the opportunity to clock teacher behaviors previously, keep this factor in mind. It will be extremely difficult to develop this skill at this point, for it takes hours of practice to time teacher behaviors in a reliable and accurate fashion. However, you should be aware that the time spent by a teacher in each category is one important consideration in analyzing classroom behavior, and you may want to devote the energy necessary to acquire this skill at a later time. Whichever techniques you choose, obtaining information about your classroom teaching behaviors represents an important step toward providing equity in the classroom and improving your teaching effectiveness.

Teaching Them All

"I have taught high school English for ten years. During that time, I have given assignments, among others, to a murderer, an evangelist, a pugilist, a thief, and an imbecile.

The murderer was a quiet boy who sat in the front row and regarded me with pale blue eyes; the evangelist, easily the most popular boy in the school, had the lead in the junior play; the pugilist lounged by the window and let loose at intervals a raucous laugh that startled even the geraniums; the thief was a gay-hearted Lothario with a song on his lips; and the imbecile, a soft-eyed little animal who sought the shadows.

The murderer awaits death in the state penitentiary; the evangelist has lain a year now in the village churchyard; the pugilist lost an eye in a brawl in Hong Kong; the thief, by standing on tiptoe, can see the windows of my room from the county jail; and the once gentle-eyed little moron beats his head against a padded wall in the state asylum.

All of these pupils once sat in my room, sat and looked at me gravely across worn brown desks. I must have been a great help to those pupils--I taught them the rhyme scheme of the Elizabethan sonnet and how to diagram a complex sentence" (26).

In "I Taught Them All," Naomi White writes with despair about her years as a teacher. All teachers have moments of futility but, at its heart, teaching is not an insignificant, paper-shuffling job. It has meaning, worth, and value. It gives you the opportunity to touch a young and impressionable life and make it better.

"We were the luckiest class in the school. We had a homeroom teacher who knew the core truth of education. Self-hate destroys, self-esteem saves. This principle guided all of her efforts on our behalf. She always minimized our deficiencies, neutralized our rage, and enhanced our natural gifts. She never, so to speak, forced a dancer to sing or a singer to dance. She allowed each of us to light his [sic] own lamp. We loved her" (7).

"Mr. Jacobs won our hearts, because he treated us as though we were already what we could only hope to become. Through his eyes we saw ourselves as capable and decent and destined for greatness. Mr. Jacobs introduced us to ourselves. We learned who we were and what we wanted to be. No longer strangers to ourselves, we felt at home in the world (7)."

You can become the kind of teacher that students will remember. Information, exercises, and observation techniques can help you become a more equitable and sensitive teacher, one who can reach all students, girls and boys. But in the end, it is your own ability, initiative, and commitment that will translate these ideas into classroom practices. By affirmative and intentional nonsexist teaching, you can treat girls and boys fairly. By eliminating stereotypes and bias from your classroom, you can introduce all of your students to who they are--and to what they are capable of becoming.

References

1. Brophy, J., and Good, T. Teacher-Student Relationships: Causes and Consequences. New York: Holt, Rinehart and Winston, 1974.

2. Casper, W. An Analysis of Sex Differences in Teacher-Student Interaction as Manifested in Verbal and Nonverbal Behavior Cues. Ph.D. dissertation, University of Tennessee, 1970.

3. Dweck, C., Davidson, W., Nelson, S., and Enna, B. Sex Differences in Learned Helplessness: II. The Contingencies of Evaluative Feedback in the Classroom and III. An Experimental Analysis. Developmental Psychology 14, pp. 268-276. 1978.

4. Dweck, C., and Gilliard, D. Expectancy Statements as Determinants of Reactions to Failure: Sex Differences in Persistence and Expectancy Change. Journal of Personality and Social Psychology 32, pp. 1077-1084. 1975.

5. Flanders, N. Analyzing Teacher Behavior. Reading, Massachusetts: Addison-Wesley, 1970.

6. Floyd, W. An Analysis of the Oral Questioning Activity in Selected Colorado Primary Classrooms. Ph.D. dissertation, Colorado State College, 1960.

7. Ginott, H. Teacher and Child. New York: Macmillan, 1972.

8. Good, T. Teacher Effectiveness in the Elementary School. Journal of Teacher Education 33, pp. 52-64. 1979.

9. Jackson, P. Life in Classrooms. New York: Holt, Rinehart and Winston, 1968.

10. Jackson, P., and Lahaderne, J. Inequalities of Teacher-Pupil Contacts. Psychology in the Schools 4, pp. 204-211. July 1967.

11. Jones, V. The Influence of Teacher-Student Introversion, Achievement and Similarity on Teacher-Student Dyadic Classroom Interactions. Ph.D. dissertation, University of Texas at Austin, 1971.

12. Kemer, B. A Study of the Relationship Between the Sex of the Student and the Assignment of Marks by Secondary School Teachers. Ph.D. dissertation, Michigan State University, 1965.

13. Knopf, S. Lessons of Consequence. Paper presented at the meeting of the American Educational Research Association, San Francisco, April 1979.

14. Palardy, J. What Teachers Believe--What Children Achieve. Elementary School Journal 69. 1969.

15. Pleck, J., and Sawyer, J. (eds.). Out in Right Field, In Men and Masculinity. Englewood Cliffs, New Jersey: Prentice-Hall, 1974.

16. Puzzles and Paradoxes: Males Dominate in Educational Success. The Educational Digest 31, pp. 11-14. January 1976.

17. Rosenthal, R., and Jacobson, L. Pygmalion in the Classroom: Teacher Expectation and Pupils' Intellectual Development. New York: Holt, Rinehart and Winston, 1968.

18. Rowe, M. Wait-Time and Rewards as Instructional Variables: Their Influence on Language, Logic and Fate Control. Paper presented at the meeting of the National Association for Research in Science Teaching. Chicago, April 1972.

19. Rubovitz, P., and Maehr, M. Pygmalion Black and White. Journal of Personality and Social Psychology 25, pp. 210-218. 1973.

20. Sears, P., and Feldman, D. Teacher Interactions with Boys and Girls. National Elementary Principal 46, pp. 30-35. November 1966.

21. Serbin, L., and O'Leary, D. How Nursery Schools Teach Girls to Shut Up. Psychology Today 9, pp. 57-58 and 102-103. 1975.

22. Serbin, L., O'Leary, K., Kent, R., and Tonick, I. A Comparison of Teacher Response to the Preacademic and Problem Behavior of Boys and Girls. Child Development 44, pp. 796-804. December 1973.

23. Sherman, J., and Fennema, E. The Study of Mathematics by High School Girls and Boys: Related Variables. American Educational Research Journal 14, pp. 159-168. Spring 1977.

24. Sikes, J. Differential Behavior of Males and Female Teachers with Male and Female Students. Ph.D. dissertation, University of Texas at Austin, 1971.

25. Spaulding, R. Achievement, Creativity, and Self-Concept Correlates of Teacher-Pupil Transactions in Elementary School. Washington, D.C.: Department of Health, Education and Welfare, 1963.

26. White, N. I Taught Them All. The Clearing House. November 1937.

Confronting Sex Bias in Instructional Materials

The National Education Association lists twenty-four different kinds of instructional materials (13).

textbooks	supplementary books
workbooks	paperbacks
pamphlets	programmed instructional systems
anthologies	dictionaries
encyclopedias	reference books
tests	classroom periodicals
newspapers	filmstrips
films	audio and video tapes
records and cassettes	slides
transparencies	globes
kits of realia	manipulative objects
learning games	graphic items (cards, posters, maps, photographs)

Categories keep growing, and the total number of learning materials now available to teachers is astonishing. There are more than a half-million different materials available for classroom use! Over twenty thousand textbook titles are mentioned in the 1977 edition of El-Hi Textbooks in Print. Another five hundred thousand nonprint titles are listed by the National Information Center for Education

---

Adapted from Sex Equity Handbook for Schools by Myra Pollack Sadker and David Miller Sadker. Coypright © 1982 by Longman Inc. Reprinted by permission.

Media (14). Instructional materials are the base of most classroom teaching with the main focus on textbooks. Research has shown that 95 percent of all teaching time is spent using some type of instructional materials, while 62.5 percent of students' classroom time is structured around print materials alone (3).

Selection Criteria

Because instructional materials are used so frequently in classrooms, their selection is critical to effective teaching. At the same time it is difficult for teachers to determine which materials might be best for their schools and classrooms because the number of available items is so large. Consequently, publishers, researchers, teachers and students are concerned with the development of criteria for selecting materials; four general criteria are generally agreed upon and should be considered (8).

1. Desirability. Do the materials meet a need? Are they appropriate for the students who will use them? Do they adhere to local social, moral, and instructional values?

2. Practicality. What are the instructional advantages and disadvantages of the materials? Are they affordable, available, easily used, and adaptable to different classrooms?

3. Intrinsic quality. Do the materials reflect equity? Are their presentations balanced in terms of sex, race, ethnicity, age, and socioeconomic level? Is the content accurate and current? Are the instructional and technical qualities adequate? Are the materials attractive and appealing to students?

4. Product development. How were the materials developed? What are the qualifications of the authors? Have the materials been evaluated? If so, how?

All of these criteria are important in the selection of instructional materials. However, this section focuses on only one aspect of textbook selection criteria: Do instructional materials reflect equity in their representation and portrayal of females and males? Although the emphasis here is on gender bias, it is important to be aware that many instructional materials reflect similar biases against racial and ethnic groups. Also, textbooks may exhibit bias against individuals or groups because of socioeconomic level, age, religion, or mental or physical handicap. The information about gender bias can be adapted to examine and counteract bias against these other groups as well.

Your Role as Instructional Decision Maker

As instructional decision maker in your classroom, you are faced with a multitude of decisions ranging from instructional style to grading policies, from methods of discipline to the physical organization of your classroom. Some of the most important decisions you make will be concerned with instructional materials. As a teacher, you may have some role in selecting the texts for your classroom, or they may be distributed to you as one of the instructional "givens" of your teaching assignment. In most cases you will be able to decide how much you wish to rely on the textbooks assigned to you. You also are likely to have a great deal of latitude in selecting a variety of materials to supplement these texts. As instructional decision maker, you are in a very influential position. You have the opportunity to combat sexism in your classroom and to develop a curriculum that encourages all students to reach their full potential.

Six Forms of Bias in Instructional Materials

Most of us have been conditioned to read information in textbooks as if it were unquestionably accurate. Consequently, it is difficult to begin reading critically to identify gender or racial bias. However, this is a necessary first step; in order to implement a gender-fair curriculum, you must first be able to recognize the biases that often exist in instructional materials.

The following pages define six different forms of gender bias. As we have mentioned, these forms of bias may also apply to racial and ethnic groups; they exist not only in textbook materials, but also in children's literature, television, movies, and many other areas as well.

Susan B. Who? Invisibility in Instructional Materials

How much do you know about the contributions made by women to the historical and contemporary development of this nation? Test your knowledge by completing the matching items in the "Susan B. Who?" quiz. (Answer key on p. 128).

Susan B. Who?

_____1. Prudence Crandall	a. An organizer of the Under ground Railroad during the Civil War
_____2. Mary Berry	b. First woman president of a major state university
_____3. Sor Juana Ines de la Cruz	c. Nuclear physicist
_____4. Patricia Harris	d. Winner of 1963 Nobel Prize for Physics
_____5. Dixie Lee Ray	e. Established a school for black girls in Connecticut prior to the Civil War
_____6. Harriet Tubman	f. Responsible for the creation of several Hispanic women's coalitions
_____7. Alice Paul	g. Classical ballet dancer of the 1940s and 1950s

_____8.	Lupe Anguiano	h.	Author of a rationale for educating women in the fifteenth century
_____9.	Susan B. Anthony	i.	Governor of Washington, former head of the Atomic Energy Commission
____10.	Betty Friedan	j.	Anthropologist, psychologist, writer, lecturer, and teacher
____11.	Maria Tallchief	k.	Leader in the struggle for women's rights during the nineteenth century
____12.	Maria Goeppert-Mayer	l.	U.S. runner who won three Olympic gold medals in 1960 for field and track
____13.	Wilma Rudolph	m.	Militant suffragist who organized parades and demonstrations in the nation's capital
____14.	Chien-Shiung Wu	n.	First black women to be appointed an ambassador and later a member of the U.S. cabinet
____15.	Margaret Mead	o.	Author of <u>The Feminine Mystique</u> and one of the founders of the National Organization for Women (NOW)

Although the women in this quiz have made significant contributions to the growth and development of this nation, few will appear in the texts that your students are assigned to read. If you were to list figures from your own study of American history, how many would be women?

Some researchers have examined textbooks to determine the number of women included and how they are portrayed. After a careful analysis of the most widely used secondary-school U.S. history texts, one researcher concluded that women arrived in 1619. They held the Seneca Falls Convention on Women's Rights in 1848. During the rest of the nineteenth century, they participated in reform movements, chiefly temperance, and were exploited in factories. In 1920 they were given the vote. They joined the armed forces during the Second World War and thereafter have enjoyed the good life in America (16).

Women suffer from such widespread omission in these texts that students typically must read over five hundred pages before they find one page of information about women (16). This form of sex bias, invisibility, characterizes not only history books, but texts in reading, language arts, mathematics, science, spelling, and vocational education.

You can examine your own textbooks for invisibility by counting the number of: (1) male-centered and female-centered examples--that is, stories or problems in which the main character is male or female; (2) males and females in illustrations; (3) males and females in various occupations; and (4) male and female biographies. This was the technique used by researchers who analyzed 134 elementary readers and reported the ratios given in the list on page 25 (18).

A 1972 study of science, math, reading, spelling, and social studies textbooks revealed that only 31 percent of all illustrations included females and that the percentage of females decreased as the grade level increased (17). This same pattern was found for illustrations of minority persons. While minorities were 33 percent of the illustrations in first-grade textbooks, they were only 26 percent at the sixth-grade level. By sixth grade, only 15 percent of the illustrations in math books and 8 percent in science books reflected minorities. The most invisible member of school texts was the minority female. Minority females appeared only half as often as minority males, and they made up only 7 percent of all females in textbooks.

Research has demonstrated that children need strong positive role models for the development of self-esteem. When females and minorities are omitted from textbooks, a hidden curriculum is created, one that teaches children that minorities and females are less important and less significant in our society than are majority males.

Can't Girls Be Exciting Too? Stereotyping in Instructional Materials

Many studies demonstrate that textbook children and adults are assigned rigid traits and roles based on their sex. This represents another form of bias--stereotyping--and it is prevalent in elementary and secondary textbooks.

Over and over again boys are portrayed as exhibiting one set of values, behaviors, and roles, and girls as exhibiting another, different set of attributes and characteristics. Researchers have found standard ways in which boys and girls are portrayed in texts (18).

Boys	Girls
ingenious	dependent
creative	passive
brave	incompetent
persevering	fearful
achieving	victimized
adventurous	docile
curious	domestic
autonomous	scorned and ridiculed
athletic	aimless
self-respecting	vain
problem solving	spiritless

A quick glance at the character lists shows that the traits are based on rigid and blatant sex-role stereotypes. Furthermore, the traits assigned to boys are generally considered more desirable and positive than are those accorded girls.

Textbook girls play with dolls, give tea parties, work in the kitchen, rarely conduct experiments, and are frightened of animals and loud noises. These girls ask advice of others and seek assistance in solving problems. In illustrations, girls are often spectators, usually watching busy, active boys at work and at play (17).

Textbook boys, on the other hand, generally participate in important activities that prepare them for the careers to be pursued as adults. They save girls and women from danger. If there is a problem to solve, they are ingenious and creative enough to find the answer. Whether they are swimming, running, riding bicycles, winning ball games, or solving mysteries, textbook boys are active and in charge.

Adult figures also suffer from sex-role stereotyping. Overwhelmingly, women are portrayed as mothers, and seldom do they work outside of the home. Textbook mothers always seem to be cooking or cleaning; in contrast, textbook fathers buy presents, take their children on trips, and in general, play with them.

Textbook occupations for women are very limited. Women are usually depicted as working in service occupations: baker, cafeteria worker, cashier, cleaning woman, cook, dressmaker, governess, housekeeper, librarian, recreational director, school crossing guard, nurse, teacher, telephone operator. Once in a while, there is a female doctor. Men are found working in approximately six times as many different occupations as are women. In a major study of elementary readers, males were found in 147 different occupations while women were found in only 26 (18).

Although males appear to be blessed with more desirable characteristics, they also suffer from stereotyping. They are expected to show emotions in real life, but in textbooks they are never allowed to cry. Although many real-life adult males change diapers, wash dishes, clean the house, and cook meals, they seldom do these things in textbooks. Some men today choose nonstereotypical careers such as nursing or preschool teaching--but not in textbooks.

In short, textbooks too often depict both males and females as sex-role stereotypes rather than as multidimensional human beings. Such stereotyping denies the reality of individual differences and prevents readers from understanding the complexity and the diversity that exists within groups.

What Struggle for Equality? Selectivity and Imbalance in Instructional Materials

Imagine that you are an author who has collected two hundred pages of notes on the second half of the nineteenth century, and this has to be reduced to one thirty-five page chapter for a U.S. history text. You must decide what is most important and should be included and what is of lesser significance and can be left out. Do you think wars and political decisions had the overwhelming influence on the development of society? Should the lives of "common people" be discussed and articulated? How much emphasis will you place on creative and artistic endeavors of the times? What reform movements deserve coverage in the thirty-five pages? As you, or any author, make such choices, another form of bias may come into play. This form is known as selectivity and imbalance.

As textbook authors decide what information to include and emphasize, the contributions of one group of people may be highlighted while those of another group may be partially or even totally omitted. For example, when the emphasis in history texts is placed on wars, the textbook characters will be primarily male. When the emphasis is placed on the role of the family or labor, the textbook characters will include more women and minorities because their contributions in these areas have been profound. If the author emphasizes the continual struggle for equality, minorities and women who led and participated in such reform movements will be recognized.

Researchers have analyzed history texts and have found that imbalance in perspective has minimized women's roles and contributions. For example, Janice Trecker studied the most widely used history texts and found that there was more information on women's skirt lengths than on the suffrage movement. In fact, the typical amount of space allotted to the struggle for women's right to vote was only a few sentences. One high school history book actually devoted a column to the Gibson girl without mentioning the suffragists of the period. The Gibson girl was described as "completely feminine, and it was clear that she could not, or would not, defeat her male companion at golf or tennis. In the event of a motoring emergency, she would quickly call upon his superior knowledge" (17).

By emphasizing the Gibson girl and omitting suffragists, this text provides an imbalanced portrayal of women's roles and contributions. It also results in a historical presentation that lacks scholarly accuracy and comprehensiveness.

Many issues, situations, and events are complex and must be viewed from a variety of perspectives. Often, authors of textbooks present only one aspect or perspective in their discussion of an event or topic. Think back to your high school history texts. Do you remember a cartoon depiction of Carry Nation, an axe-carrying temperance movement leader? As a result of that caricature you may think of the temperance movement as ridiculous. While highlighting the activities of Carry Nation, your text may not have stressed the reasons for the temperance movement. Families of alcoholic men suffered devastating abuse; wives had little recourse in such situations; divorces were difficult to obtain and economic opportunities for women were severely limited. To caricature the temperance movement without providing a discussion about why it occurred represents only one aspect of a very serious problem. This is another example of bias through selectivity and imbalance.

This form of bias is harmful not only to the presentation of women, but to that of other minorities as well. History texts have focused primarily on the origins and heritage of European settlers in this nation. The voluntary and nonvoluntary immigration of other groups is given little attention. The relationships between the federal government and native Americans are usually examined only from the government's perspective in terms of treaties and "protection"; a native American perspective would also examine broken treaties and appropriation of native lands.

The selectivity and imbalance found in textbooks is unfair to students. It prevents females and minority group members from realizing that they have contributed significantly to the development of our society. It prevents all students from realizing the complexity of historical and contemporary situations and developments.

On the Sunny Side of the Page: Unreality in Instructional Materials

One-half of the nation's work force is female, and 90 percent of all women will work outside the home at some time during their lives. Moreover, 35 percent of these working women have children under eighteen. Many working mothers travel on business trips and take their families on vacation. In reality, the traditional roles of men and women are in flux. Both men and women today work in a variety of careers and share many formerly gender-typed roles and activities. But this change is not reflected in most textbooks. Textbooks' failure to reflect accurately the contemporary and changing nature of men's and women's roles represents another form of bias, that of unreality. Texts reflect unreality not only when they fail to recognize social change, but also when they gloss over or even completely ignore controversial and troublesome issues. Many of these changes and issues involve women and minorities.

For example, consider the textbook housewife, a truly amazing character. Well-groomed and protected by a spotless apron, she smoothly organizes her household world; she is invariably happy and calm. The realities of caring for children and husband, cleaning, cooking, shopping, doing laundry, repairing a leaky faucet, entertaining, chauffeuring, and bookkeeping are not presented. Nor is the difficult juggling act of combining a career and the care of home and children.

Let us broaden the focus to consider the typical textbook family--mother, father, older son, younger daughter, and dog called Spot. In real life over 30 percent of the families in this nation are headed by a single parent, and one of every 17 American children lives in a single-parent family. But these nontraditional families are rarely seen in textbooks, and the issue of divorce is seldom presented.

Textbooks also reflect unreality when they ignore controversial or unpleasant issues such as racism, sexism, prejudice, discrimination, and intergroup conflict. Contemporary problems of minorities and women are often glossed over. For example, textbooks typically provide only historical information on native Americans. There is far less discussion of the devastating problems faced by this group today. There is also little discussion of sexual and racial bias in employment and in salaries.

Obviously the achievements and successes of the United States should be presented in textbooks. But problems and difficulties must be analyzed as well. When controversial issues are not presented, students are denied the information they need to confront contemporary problems and to work toward their resolution.

Woman in a Box: Fragmentation and Isolation in Instructional Materials

Have you ever opened a book and found a section set off from the regular text by different-colored type or boxed-off lines? These sections may have had titles such as "Ten Distinguished Black Americans" or "Susan B. Anthony: An Early Feminist." Such treatment results in another form of bias, fragmentation and isolation.

Texts reflect this form of bias when they isolate information pertaining to women and minorities from the main body of the text. Publishers often include these separate boxes, sections, or chapters in an attempt to update their books and incorporate previously omitted information. Obviously, it is much less expensive to insert these add-ons than to integrate women and minorities throughout the text.

However, isolating information sends negative messages to students; it suggests that the experiences and contributions of women and minorities are merely interesting diversions, but they are not integral to the mainstream of historical and contemporary developments in our society.

It probably sounds like an easy matter to spot fragmentation and isolation in texts--a simple check for a separate box or a section on women. Actually, it is more complex. You should be aware that if information about women and minorities is integrated throughout the text, then a separate section may actually serve to highlight their contributions. However, if pertinent information is not woven throughout the textbook, then a separate section or box does reflect this form of bias.

Fragmentation and isolation also occur when women and minority groups are depicted as interacting only among themselves and having little or no influence on society as a whole. For example, textbook discussions of feminism often talk about how women are affected by this contemporary movement; typically there is little analysis of the impact of the women's movement on other groups and social issues. Such treatment of women and minorities in textbooks implies that their history, their experiences, and their contributions are insignificant to the development of contemporary society.

Will People Replace Mankind? Linguistic Bias in Materials

It is time to change pace for a minute--get out your sketchbook and draw a picture of an early caveman. Try to reflect in your drawing the kinds of activities he was involved in, the types of implements he used, and what his life may have been like.

Examine what you drew. Is your early caveman male or female? What are the activities and implements you depicted?

Caveman is supposedly a generic term used to refer to all persons living during our earliest history. However, studies show that when elementary-school children are asked to draw pictures of early cavemen, they do what they are told. They draw men. On the other hand, when they are asked to draw early cave people, they also do what they are told. They draw people--men, women, children, family groupings. In short, masculine nouns--caveman, mankind, forefathers--and masculine pronouns are not as generic as we once thought. When children hear or read them, they may not form images of all people. Rather, they take the terms literally; when they read he and man, they think male.

A similar process occurs with occupational terms. When texts mention policemen, firemen, salesmen, or businessmen, children may not realize that these terms are supposed to include everyone. As a result, they may consider a wide range of occupational aspirations to be inappropriate for girls.

Table 3
Nonsexist Alternatives for Some Common Words and Phrases

Common Word	Nonsexist Replacements
mankind	humanity, human beings, human race, people
primitive man	primitive people, primitive men and women
man-made	artificial, synthetic, manufactured
congressman	member of Congress, representative
businessman	business executive, business manager
fireman	fire fighter
mailman	mail carrier, letter carrier
salesman	sales representative, sales person, sales clerk
insurance man	insurance agent
statesman	leader, public servant
chairman	presiding officer, the chair, head, leader, coordinator, chair-person, moderator
policeman	police officer, officer

Another form of linguistic bias occurs when women are referred to as someone's wife or possession: "Phillip Lau took his wife to Chicago." Or, "The pioneer and his wife, children, and cattle moved West." When this is reworded, "The pioneer family moved West," all members of the family become associated with the traits of ingenuity, bravery, and courage--not just the pioneer male.

While language reflects the biases of society, it is probably the easiest form of bias to change in textbooks. Language is the area most frequently addressed by commercial publishers who have developed guidelines for improving the image of women in books. Changing language alone will not greatly alter the way women are perceived by readers, but such change is one positive way to begin. On the other hand, continued use of sexist terms and predominantly male references can only reinforce gender biases that exist in other forms.

Can you recognize the six forms of bias in instructional materials? Let's recap each form (11).

1. Invisibility. Certain groups are underrepresented in curricular materials. The significant omission of women and minority groups has become so great that it implies that these groups are of less value, importance, and significance in our society.

2. Stereotyping. By assigning traditional and rigid roles or attributes to a group, instructional materials stereotype and limit the abilities and potential of that group. Stereotyping denies students knowledge of the diversities, complexities, and variations in groups of individuals. Children who see themselves portrayed only in stereotypic ways may internalize these stereotypes and fail to develop their own unique abilities, interests, and full potential.

3. Imbalance and selectivity. Textbooks perpetuate bias by presenting only one interpretation of an issue, situation, or group of people. This imbalanced account restricts a student's knowledge. Through selective presentation of materials, textbooks distort reality and ignore complex and differing viewpoints. As a result, millions of students have limited perspectives about contributions, struggles, and participation of women and minorities in our society.

4. Unreality. Textbooks frequently present an unrealistic portrayal of our history and our contemporary life experience. Controversial topics are glossed over and discussions of discrimination and prejudice are avoided. This unrealistic coverage denies children the information they need to recognize, understand, and perhaps someday conquer the problems that plague our society.

5. Fragmentation and isolation. By separating issues related to minorities and women from the main body of the text, instructional materials imply that these issues are less important than and not a part of the cultural mainstream.

6. Linguisitic bias. Curricular materials reflect the discriminatory nature of our language. Masculine terms

and pronouns deny the participation of women in our society. Further, certain occupations are given masculine labels, which deny the legitimacy of women working in these fields. Imbalance of word order and lack of parallel terms to refer to females and males are also forms of linguistic bias.

At this point you may be thinking that immersion in the day-to-day realities of teaching does not allow time for this kind of textbook analysis. It is true that textbook analysis is not a quick, easy task; however, as you continue to practice your skills you will find the process becoming far less cumbersome and time consuming. Also, schools and organizations have developed a variety of aids to help you evaluate your classroom instructional materials for sexual and racial biases:

Biased Textbooks: Action Steps You Can Take. The Resource Center on Sex Equity, Council for Chief State School Officers, 400 North Capitol St., Suite 379, Washington, D.C. 20001.

Dick and Jane as Victims: Sex Stereotyping in Children's Readers. Women on Words and Images, P.O. Box 2163, Princeton, New Jersey 08540.

Equal Treatment of Sexes in Social Studies Textbooks: Guidelines for Authors and Editors. Westside Women's Committee, Box 24020, Village Station, Los Angeles, California 90022.

How Fair Are Your Children's Textbooks? National Education Association, Publications Order Department, Academic Building, Saw Mill Rd., West Haven, Connecticut 06516.

Sex Equality in Educational Materials. (AASA Executive Handbook Series #4 American Association of School Administrators, 1801 N. Moore St., Arlington, Virginia 22209.

Stereotypes, Distortions and Omissions in U.S. History Textbooks. Racism and Sexism Resource Center for Educators, 1841 Broadway, New York, New York 10023.

Ten Quick Ways to Analyze Children's Books for Racism and Sexism. Council on Interracial Books for Children, 1841 Broadway, New York, New York 10023.

Beyond Pictures and Pronouns: Sexism in Teacher Education Textbooks. Education Development Center, 55 Chapel St., Newton, Massachusetts 02160.

The Impact of Bias in Books

You may be saying that perhaps gender bias does exist in classroom materials; but can this really affect my students? Can bias in books promote sexist or racist attitudes and behaviors? Or is this bias only an annoying remnant of bygone days without real significance for today's students and teachers?

According to a number of studies, bias in books cannot be dismissed as merely insignificant or annoying (19). Students at various grade levels report that they have changed their attitudes and behaviors as a result of their reading. Changes occur in self-image, philosophy of life, interpersonal sensitivity, and opinions toward different cultural groups and social problems (4). Therefore, if books distort or stereotype a certain group, this misrepresentation can affect student attitudes and perceptions. Here is how the process works. If you are a member of minority group or a female, or both, you may find yourself turning page after page before you find a character who represents you. Unfortunately, when minority and female characters do appear, they frequently have only minimal, stereotypic roles. As a female or minority reader, you are probably receiving a clear message that you are not as worthy or as important as others, and your self-image might be negatively affected.

But this need not be the case. Researchers have also found that books can have a positive influence on children. Several studies indicate that multicultural and nonsexist reading materials have a positive effect on children's attitudes toward minority-group members and other children (2). For example, one study showed that black and white children demonstrated much more favorable attitudes toward blacks following exposure to multicultural readers (10). Another study indicated that both boys and girls in grades one through five developed less stereotyped attitudes about jobs and activities after reading about people who successfully fought sex discrimination in nontraditional jobs (15).

Not by the Book Alone

Obviously, books alone do not create attitudes. Children arrive at the schoolhouse door with a host of values and opinions that they have adopted or adapted from parents, friends, television, and other sources. In fact, studies reveal that both children and adults tend to interpret what they read so that it will conform to their previously internalized attitudes and behaviors (12). For example, a child who holds stereotypic attitudes about the roles of men and women will tend to recall characters in books who demonstrate sex-stereotypic traits (9).

This does not mean that nonsexist books are ineffective; it suggests that books alone may not make the difference. Books are only one component, although an important one, in the overall instructional program that you will have to implement in order to promote sex equity in your classroom. For example, one six-week project focused on children in kindergarten, and in fifth and ninth grades. Teachers used nonsexist books and other materials to encourage these students to develop nonsexist attitudes and behaviors. Evaluation of this nonsexist-curriculum project revealed that many of the girls showed an improvement in their self-esteem and acceptance of the wide range of options available to them as adults. However, one of the most significant findings of this study was that teacher enthusiasm was a key factor in affecting attitudinal change in boys and girls at all levels. Enthusiastic teachers used the materials more, and their students' attitudes were more likely to shift to egalitarian views (7). These findings suggest that nonsexist books alone may not be enough to influence a change in attitudes. Teachers who positively and enthusiastically use nonsexist materials play a very important role in reducing or eliminating children's sex-role stereotypes.

You've Come a Short Way, Publisher!
What Publishers Have and Have Not Done about Gender Bias

Now that you understand how gender bias in educational materials can have a very real and injurious effect on students, your response is probably going to be, What is being done about this problem and how can I, as a teacher, change the situation? Obviously, one of the ways to deal with gender bias in textbooks is to try to influence publishers to make changes. This is not as easy as it sounds.

The 1972 publication Dick and Jane as Victims called national attention to gender bias in children's readers. A number of women's groups and other organizations were making similar discoveries across the nation as they investigated the textbooks used in their local schools. With the pressure and publicity of such studies, most major publishing companies developed and disseminated guidelines for the preparation of nonsexist materials. Scott, Foresman was the first company to publish guidelines to improve the image of women in textbooks (5). Four key points of these guidelines follow.

1. The actions and achievements of women should be recognized.
2. Women and girls should be given the same respect as men and boys.
3. Abilities, traits, interests, and activities should not be assigned on the basis of male or female stereotypes.
4. Sexist language should be avoided.

The guidelines developed by Holt, Rinehart and Winston outlined three areas that should be addressed for a more equitable treatment of sex roles (6).

1. Role Models. The traditional roles of women in society as homemakers and in the areas of child rearing, education, nursing, and the arts are both valuable and vital to the life of society. No effort should be made to downgrade or disparage these roles. Rather, an effort must be made to expand the roles of both sexes, to include men in nurturing and homemaking activities and to include women in areas such as business and science. An unbalanced assignment of such roles does a disservice to both sexes. Children should see people of both sexes in a variety of those models and thus develop their own individual talents and preferences to their best advantage.

2. <u>Subject Matter</u>. Educational materials should acknowledge the roles and contributions of both women and men. Materials that do not meet these criteria or that are biased in language or in attitude should be avoided wherever possible.

3. <u>Language</u>. Careful and sensitive use of language is important in achieving a positive tone and in creating balance.

A list of publishers' guidelines for the preparation of nonsexist material follows.

<u>Avoiding Stereotypes</u>. Houghton Mifflin Co., College Division, 1 Beacon Street, Boston, Massachusetts 02107.

<u>Guidelines for Creating Positive Sexual and Racial Images in Educational Materials</u>. Macmillan Publishing Co., 866 Third Ave., New York, New York 10022.

<u>Guidelines for the Development of Elementary and Secondary Instructional Materials</u>. Holt, Rinehart and Winston, 383 Madison Ave., New York, New York 10017.

<u>Guidelines for Eliminating Stereotypes from Instructional Material Grades K-12</u>. Harper & Row, School Department, 10 East 53rd Street, New York, New York 10022.

<u>Guidelines for Equal Treatment of the Sexes in McGraw-Hill Book Company Publications</u>. McGraw-Hill, 1221 Avenue of the Americas, New York, New York 10020.

<u>Guidelines for Improving the Image of Women in Textbooks</u>. Scott, Foresman & Co., 1900 East Lake Avenue, Glenview, New York 60025.

<u>Statement on Bias-Free Materials</u>. Association of American Publishers, School Division, One Park Avenue, New York, NY 10016.

<u>Suggestions for Developing Materials That Are Free of Racial, Sexual, Cultural and Social Bias</u>. Science Research Associates, 259 East Erie Street, Chicago, Illinois 60611.

What Publishers Have Not Done

Unfortunately, the new editions of textbooks have not fulfilled the promise of the publisher's guidelines. Researchers have found that the language itself is not as blatantly masculine as it once was, but the number of male-centered stories has increased rather than decreased! Female central stories and illustrations are still very few. Ethnic minority males made the largest gain as characters in stories and in illustrations, but minority females remain almost nonexistent. And the newer texts still provide little about the historical reality of women's experiences and achievements.

In the everyday practice of teaching, we are often so busy we do not have time to review textbooks carefully. In quick "thumb-through" evaluations, we might be impressed by the changes we see. However, a more thorough examination would reveal that these changes are superficial rather than substantive. Some of the techniques publishers are using to make cosmetic rather than significant textbook changes include inserts, cosmetic or color changes, names and pronoun changes, story clustering and increased neuter-character stories.

New materials are added to a text, usually in the center or at the end of the book. These materials often appear as add-ons because they are inconsistent with the original book format. When cosmetic or color changes are made, the same characters of previous editions are colored to appear black or tan. Sometimes the features are changed to match the corresponding ethnic groups, but sometimes the features remain Anglo.

To make name and pronoun changes, an Anglo name is changed to an ethnic name without changing the cultural context of the story (e.g., Robert to Roberto). The same technique is used to change the sex of the character (e.g., Paul to Pauline). Researchers found that the stories in which such changes were made were characterized as the weaker stories, those in which the main characters were less admirable or heroic.

Publishers are guilty of story clustering when female- or minority-centered stories are added or substituted in only one or two books of a series at only one grade level rather than in all of the books in the series at various grade levels. And, neuter-character syndrome is an increase in the proportion of stories about neuter animals and objects, which causes the deletion of both male and female characters. What is needed is an increase of female characters, not more neuter stories (1).

Researchers who have analyzed the newer texts conclude that "textbook companies which have published guidelines for reducing sexism and racism are to be congratulated for publishing excellent guidelines, yet criticized for failure to follow them. They have examined the issues and outlined some pioneering and innovative ideas for change for themselves and the entire textbook industry. What they have failed to demonstrate are "good-faith" attempts to implement their own guidelines"(1).

The Excuse for No Change

Understandably, textbook publishers expect to make a profit from their sales of textbooks. This, however, has become the excuse for not making textbooks as equitable or representative as they should be. When confronted with their snail-paced rate of change, the common response has been that such revisions are financially prohibitive.

As long as school districts continue to buy sexist textbooks, publishers will produce them. The profit motive encourages these companies to appeal to the largest possible market. Consequently, they will make some changes to indicate sensitivity to racism and sexism. At the same time, they worry about the possibility of fewer sales in very conservative areas of the country where there is antagonism toward such change.

Local groups or individuals can encourage textbook reform. They can exert influence and pressure so that schools will not purchase racist and sexist books. Only when educators, parents, and textbook publishers work cooperatively to eliminate sexism and racism will we begin to see instructional materials that are truly representative of the world's diversity.

What You Can Do in Your Classroom

If the textbooks you are given to use with students are biased, it is important to confront this bias rather than to ignore it. A natural and legitimate way to begin this process is simply to level with your students. It is entirely appropriate to acknowledge that texts are not always perfect. You can engage your students in a discussion about textbook omission and stereotyping. You may find that many students are initially reluctant to challenge any information housed between textbook covers; however, if you handle these discussions sensitively and constructively, you may find that you are developing their critical and analytical reading skills as well.

Being honest and direct with your students about bias in instructional material provides a way to begin, but it is crucial that you go beyond simply calling attention to omission, stereotyping, and other forms of bias. It is not enough to recognize, for example, that there are few women in the classroom history text. Some students may remain skeptical, claiming that this is probably because women have done little worth recording. Other students in your class may believe that history texts are biased, but they may be unaware of the nature and extent of this bias. In order to develop students' awareness, it will be up to you to supply the information that has been omitted from or distorted in your classroom text. This will inform the cynical students as well as the committed ones.

That's quite a tall order, you are more than likely thinking. You may yourself be unaware of the contributions and history of women simply because you have not been exposed to that information in your own school experience. Trying to fill these gaps may seem like an overwhelming assignment. Where do you begin?

Fortunately, there are a number of individuals and organizations concerned and angry about bias in texts; they have begun the production of supplementary information that should be in your texts.

Building Fairness Resource Center
Vocational Education Studies Department
Rehn Hall 135a
Southern Illinois University
Carbondale, Illinois 62901
(800)624-5592 (Illinois only)
(618)453-3321 Ext. 241

The Building Fairness Resource Center serves as a clearinghouse for sex-equity-related resources in Illinois. The Center houses an extensive collection of audiovisual and print materials suitable for many ages and groups. The resources are available to educators on a free-loan basis.

The Center has also developed a nontraditional role-model directory that lists persons in Illinois who are employed in nontraditional occupations and careers for their sex. Requests for this directory and requests for information or assistance may be made by calling the Resource Center.

Consortium for Educational Equity
Rutgers, The State University
Kilmer Campus 4090
New Brunswick, New Jersey 08903
(201)932-2071 or 2072

The Consortium for Educational Equity at Rutgers University has developed excellent resources that promote nontraditional career choices. Included is the Futures Unlimited series of videotapes and posters which depict women in nontraditional occupations. Order information is available upon request.

Council on Interracial Books for Children
Racism and Sexism Resource Center for Educators
1841 Broadway
New York, New York 10023
(212)757-5339

The Council on Interracial Books publishes and produces a variety of multiethnic and nonsexist materials for elementary and secondary schools and libraries. Its publication, The Bulletin, comes out eight times a year and includes children's book reviews and articles about sexism and special needs of children in education. A free catalog is available upon request.

Education Development Center
55 Chapel Street
Newton, Massachusetts 02160
(800)225-3088
(617)969-7100

The Education Development Center (EDC) serves as the dissemination center for programs and products developed under the Women's Educational Equity Act Program (WEEAP). A catalog describing materials can be obtained from EDC at no cost. It can assist school personnel in determining product applicability for specific program needs.

The Feminist Press
SUNY/College of Old Westbury
Box 334
Old Westbury, New York 11568
(516)997-7660

The Feminist Press is a nonprofit, educational organization that publishes nonsexist books, curriculum materials and outlines, resource lists, anthologies, bibliographies, biographies, children's books, and reprints of important and neglected women's writings for every educational level. In addition, the press sponsors a clearinghouse for information about nonsexist education and Title IX. It also conducts teacher and administrator workshops on the use of nonsexist educational materials and strategies.

General Electric Company
Educational Communications Programs
Fairfield, Connecticut 06431
(203)373-2030

General Electric offers a "World of Work" kit, which consists of a series of eye-catching posters that invite students to correlate interests and abilities with areas of work. In addition, career education booklets, such as "Planning Your Career", "So You Want to Go to Work?", "What's It Like to Be an Engineer?" are available.

These world-of-work materials are nonsexist and portray many persons in nontraditional activities. Copies of these materials, which are especially useful for junior and senior high school students, have been widely distributed. If your school does not have a set, single copies are available and free.

Girls Clubs of America, Inc.
National Resource Center
441 West Michigan St.
Indianapolis, Indiana 46202
(800)428-4224

The Girls Clubs of America (GCA) National Resource Center serves as a clearinghouse for information on girls' needs and concerns and the best programs to meet them. All GCA publications and audiovisual materials are distributed through the National Resource Center and may be ordered by schools, individuals, researchers, or parents. Titles include "Facts and Reflections on Careers for Today's Girls" and "Operation SMART," a program that encourages girls in science, math, and technology.

Math/Science Network
Math/Science Resource Center
Mills College
Oakland, California 94613
(415)430-2230

The Math/Science Network was established to promote the participation of girls and women in mathematics and science and to encourage their entry into nontraditional occupations. At the Resource Center at Mills College the staff provides strategies and "how-to" materials to public-school personnel for increasing the number of young women in math and science careers. They disseminate information through the local math/science network. Resources can be obtained from the Education Development Center. An award-winning videotape "Nothing But Options" is available for rent or purchase from the Math/Science Network.

National Women's History Project
P.O. Box 3716
Santa Rosa, California 95402
(707)526-5974

The National Women's History Project is the originator and primary promoter of National Women's History Week/Month. As part of their service, they are a mail-order source for current books, posters, and curriculum materials that promote the inclusion of women's history in K-12 curricula. In addition to the resource service, the National Women's History Project has developed a consulting service. Their in-service training workshops and three-day curriculum conferences introduce educators to the resources and teaching strategies available to integrate women's history into the curriculum.

TABS: Aids for Ending Sexism in School
744 Carroll Street
Brooklyn, New York 11215
(212)788-3478

TABS is a quarterly journal that includes practical aids for equal education of the sexes. The journal has published posters and biographies of Fannie Lou Hamer and Marie Curie, lesson plans on such issues as "How should you decide who does household chores?", and feature articles such as "Girls and Science Careers: A Program for Change," and "How to Run a Susan B. Anthony Day in Your School." In addition to feature articles, every issue contains display items for the classroom, ideas for nonsexist activities, lesson plans, reviews of curricula and other materials, instructional materials, evaluations, and biographies of women of achievement. Subscriptions are available, and posters may be purchased separately.

These supplementary materials will provide you with a bonanza of exciting and informative classroom lessons. The resource materials can be used as supplements to your textbook, which may not be meeting the needs of all of your students--the treatment of women is a prime example of this failure. You may wish to prepare discussions, lectures, fact sheets, case studies, or other classroom activities based on the supplementary materials. In some cases, you can distribute the materials directly to the students as reading assignments. In other situations, you will want to serve as a mediator and present them through classroom discussions and activities. Either approach provides students with ideas and information that go beyond the limits of textbooks currently available.

The day-to-day realities of the classroom are hectic and pressured, and you cannot and should not be expected to spend hour after hour continually researching and preparing supplementary materials. However, through research, writing, and presentation assignments, you can share this learning responsibility with your students. If you do an effective job of calling attention to text bias and of stimulating students' curiosity about the women and other minorities who are missing from textbook pages, you can motivate students to undertake independent work, to conduct their own research, and to prepare original reports and papers, work that can be shared with the entire class to raise everyone's consciousness on these issues.

Although the initial response of many teachers concerned about the limitations of their texts is to seek other printed materials as supplementary resources, there is no reason to limit supplemental materials in this way. Many organizations will provide guest speakers for your class. Others have developed slide-tape presentations, posters, and films that are motivating and informative. Using this wealth of audiovisual materials and guest speakers can be an asset to your classroom and can enhance the awareness of your students about sex equity.

As a teacher, the instructional decision maker in your classroom, you will be the one to determine how you will use classroom materials. You can accept biased books as "instructional givens," or you can work with your students to analyze, confront, and change these biases. The opportunity and the challenge are yours.

References

1. Britton, G., and Lumpkin M. A Consumer's Guide to Sex, Race, and Career Bias in Public School Textbooks. Corvallis, Oregon: Britton and Assoc., 1977.

2. Campbell, P., and Wirtenburg, J. How Books Influence Children: What the Research Shows. Interracial Books for Children Bulletin 11. 1980.

3. EPIE Institute. Report on a National Study of the Nature and the Quality of Instructional Materials Most Used by Teachers and Learners. New York, 1977.

4. Guidelines for Improving the Image of Women in Textbooks. Glenview, Illinois: Scott, Foresman, 1972.

5. Guidelines for the Development of Elementary and Secondary Instructional Materials. New York: Holt, Rinehart and Winston, 1975.

6. Guttentag, M., and Bray, H. Undoing Sex Stereotypes: Research and Resources for Educators. New York: McGraw-Hill, 1976.

7. Klein, S. Toward Consensus on Minimum Criteria for Educational Products. Paper presented at American Educational Ressearch Association Annual Meeting. San Francisco, April 1976.

8. Koblinsky, S., Cruse, D., and Sugawara, A. Sex Role Stereotypes and Children's Memory for Story Content. Child Development 49, pp. 452-458. 1978.

9. Litcher, J., and Johnson, D. Changes in Attitudes Toward Negroes of White Elementary School Students after Use of Multiethnic Readers. Journal of Educational Psychology 60, pp. 148-152. April 1969.

10. McCune, S., and Mathews, M. Implementing Title IX and Attaining Sex Equity: A Workshop Package for Postsecondary Educators. Washington, D.C.: U.S. Government Printing Office, 1978. TEW-3.

11. McKillip, A. The Relationship Between the Reader's Attitudes and Certain Types of Reading Responses. New York: Teacher's College, Columbia University, 1972.

12. National Education Association. Instructional Materials, Selection and Purchase. Washington, D.C.: National Education Association, 1976.

13. National Institute of Education. Toward Improving National Efforts Related to Instructional Materials Selection. Report to NIE. Washington, D.C., June 1977.

14. Scott, K. Elementary Pupils' Perceptions of Reading and Social Studies Materials: Does the Sex of the Main Character Make a Difference? Dissertation Abstracts UMI 780973. Ann Anbor, 1977.

15. Shirley, F. The Influence of Reading on Concepts, Attitudes, and Behavior. Journal of Reading, pp. 369-372 and 407-413. February 1969.

16. Trecker, J. Women in U.S. History High School Textbooks. In Sex Bias in the Schools: The Research Evidence, Pottker and Fishel (eds.). Cranbury, New Jersey: Associated University Presses, 1977.

17. Weitzman, L., and Rizzo, D. Biased Textbooks. Washington, D.C.: Resource Center on Sex Roles in Education, 1974.

18. Women on Words and Images. Dick and Jane as Victims: Sex Stereotyping in Children's Readers. Washington, D.C.: Resource Center on Sex Roles in Education, 1974.

19. Zimet, S. Print and Prejudice. London: Hodder and Stoughton, in association with the United Kingdom Reading Association, 1976.

Answer Key: Susan B. Who?

1. e	2. b	3. h	4. n	5. i
6. a	7. m	8. f	9. k	10. o
11. g	12. d	13. l	14. c	15. j

The Influence of Parents on the Educational and Occupational Decision Making of Their Children

Although gains have been made in the reduction of sex-role stereotyping and gender bias, there still exists a need for improvement. Females continue to dominate the traditionally female classes and occupations, and males continue to dominate the traditionally male classes and occupations. Several studies have identified the influential people in the educational and occupational decision-making process for youth.

Influential People in Occupational Choice

Studies indicate that a student's mother had the greatest influence on post-high-school plans for seniors followed closely by the student's father. Friends, teachers, and counselors were less influential. Parents and peers are very important in pressuring young women toward traditional vocational courses. This pressure--combined with lack of information on specific employment opportunities, lack of preparation in certain skills, and lack of encouragement by counselors and school personnel--constitutes the major barrier females face in access to nontraditional classes and careers.

Counselors and administrators tend to reinforce stereotypical behavior in male and female students. As a result, the differential treatment students receive reduces the career options that students see as available and

---

Adapted from a paper of the same title by T. Erekson and P. Young.

appropriate. The barriers males and females face in entering nontraditional classes are not only a result of other people--external--but can become internal. That is, students' fear of their peers' reactions becomes a motivating force behind their educational choices.

Parents, peers, teachers, counselors, and siblings are the people the student looks to for guidance, knowledge, encouragement, approval, and acceptance. They have the greatest opportunities to serve as influential forces in the career-decision-making process.

Parental Influence

The majority of research on the significant people during a student's choice of occupation focuses on the importance of parents. Students enrolled in traditional courses for their sex stated that parents and counselors were more important than peers in influencing their occupational program. Career development starts early in childhood and continues throughout life, and parents are a significant factor in this developmental process. Parents are the primary people in a child's life in the early years, and along with educators and peers, continue to be important throughout adolescence. In the elementary years, children look to parents for approval and as role models. Parents provide a vast amount of information about life and the roles of males and females within society through spoken and written words, and through their actions.

Because the child spends the majority of his or her formative years with parents (family), the child uses these individuals as his or her references for the "typical" roles and behaviors males and females should assume. They look at how the parents treat each other, the other children, and males and females outside the family unit. The child will then incorporate these attitudes and actions into his or her own value system through the socialization process. There is a tendency for children to associate an occupation with one gender, and they are strongly influenced by their parents' occupations, beliefs, and attitudes. This is not unusual, due to the child's limited access to adult role models, but it is critical because it is their first exposure to what his or her role(s) will be in society.

Parents can broaden their child's knowledge of careers. Most children will not on their own seek all of the possible options, but they will listen to a role model relate career information. Parents can be major providers of career information to their children if they are given adequate training and materials and if they understand their child's skills, abilities, and interests.

The mother's influence. The majority of research concerning parental influence has examined the mother as a role model. Studies indicate that the attitudes and beliefs of the mother are influential in the career choice of the daughters. But not only are attitudes and beliefs important, but several researchers have emphasized the importance of the working mother (employed outside of the home) on career choices. Working mothers are more likely to have daughters who choose to work, and the daughter's career choice is likely to be similar to the mother's career. Studies of the female who expected to be a homemaker and not employed outside the home revealed a significant relationship between the nonemployed mother and the female who saw herself as a homemaker at age thirty.

While much of the research on the mother focused on only the daughter, studies show that sons and daughters of employed mothers have fewer sex-stereotyped expectations and values than children of mothers who are not employed. Sons will see other females as being capable of securing a job, of contributing to society, and of being a provider as well.

The father's influence. Just as a relationship exists for the mother and daughter in career choice, research has identified the father-son relationship as important in career choice. There is a tendency for the son to select a career similar to his father's career. Not only the occupation, but also the values the father has toward work may influence the son's vocational choice. The closeness of the relationship between the father and son is also an important variable.

Studies indicate that certain types of fathers' occupations are associated with similar types of career choices by sons. For example, sons of fathers who are in teaching or guidance are likely to select careers in teaching, in administration, in the church, or in social work, or if the father is in the medical field, the son is likely to choose a medical career. Boys' career objectives identify more with their fathers' occupation than girls' with their mothers'. Some studies have analyzed the importance of the father in influencing the educational and career plans of the daughter. As with the mother, the father's attitude is very important--he can serve as an encourager or discourager for his daughter's pursuit of a traditional or nontraditional career. The female may choose a nontraditional occupation but her decision is influenced by her immediate environment. One of these environmental factors is the father's attitude. His perception of women in the work force and the relation of his perception to his daughter, can be a positive or negative influence on her future career plans.

A survey of parents revealed that while some were in favor of traditional class enrollments, a larger percentage indicated support for the nontraditional male or female student than the actual percentage of males and females currently enrolled in these nontraditional courses. The daughter is not only influenced by encouragement and support from the father, but will look to him as a role model. He will influence her in a positive direction if he is an achieving role model.

Conclusions

Several conclusions can be drawn from this review of the research on influences affecting the career choice for males and females.

1. Parents are the most influential people in the occupational and educational decision making of their children.

2. Parental encouragement is highly significant in influencing children toward nontraditional careers.

3. Parents are seen as role models by their children, and they either promote or hinder their children's choices of traditional or nontraditional classes and careers.

4. One way to begin breaking down barriers for males and females in selecting and entering nontraditional classes and careers is to give the parents and children factual employment-opportunity information, inform them of the

necessary skills, abilities, and aptitudes for various careers; and help parents see their roles as models in the career choices of their children.

References

1. Auster, C., and Auster, D. Factors Influencing Women's Choice of Nontraditional Careers: The Role of Family, Peers, and Counselors. Vocational Guidance Quarterly, pp. 253-263. March 1981.

2. Burlin, E. The Relationship of Parental Education and Maternal Work and Occupational Status to Occupational Aspiration in Adolescent Females. Journal of Vocational Behavior, pp. 99-103. August 1978.

3. Church, O. Career Objectives of Wyoming Secondary Students Compared with Parental Occupations. Cheyenne: Wyoming State Department of Education. August 1974.

4. Falkowski, C., and Falk, W. Homemaking as an Occupational Plan: Evidence from a National Longitudinal Study. Journal of Vocational Behavior 22, pp. 227-242. April 1983.

5. Haber, S. Cognitive Support for the Career Choices of College Women. Sex Roles: A Journal of Research, pp. 129-138. February 1980.

6. Hotchkiss, L., and Chiteji, L. The Dynamics of Career Expectations of Youth: A Theoretical Formulation and Empirical Report Based on a Longitudinal Study. Columbus: Ohio State University, National Center for Research in Vocational Education. 1981.

7. Lamb, M. Nontraditional Families: Parenting and Child Development. Hillsdale, New Jersey: Lawrence Erlbaum Assoc., 1982.

8. Lunneborg, P. Role-Model Influencers on Nontraditional Professional Women. Journal of Vocational Behavior, pp. 276-281. June 1982.

9. Mills, M. The Influence of Parent's Occupation on the Career Choice of Vocationally Undecided Youth. Quebec, Canada, 1980.

10. Mortimer, J. Patterns of Intergenerational Occupational Movements: A Smallest-Space Analysis. American Journal of Sociology, pp. 1278-1299. March 1974.

11. Navin, S., and Sears, S. Parental Roles in Elementary Career Guidance. Elementary School Guidance and Counseling, pp. 269-277. April 1980.

12. Sandler, R. When I Was Little I Didn't Know Girls Could Do That. Women in Skilled Trades. June 1982.

13. Snell, M. Trying Out Male Roles for Size. American Vocational Journal 52, pp. 59-60. may 1977.

14. Stevens, G., and Body, M. The Importance of Mother: Labor Force Participation and Intergenerational Mobility of Women. Social Forces, pp. 186-199. September 1980.

15. Veres, H., and Carmichael, M. Expanding Student Opportunities in Occupational Education: Methods to Reduce Sex-Role Stereotyping in Program Choice. Ithaca, New York: State University of New York, Cornell Institute for Occupational Education, 1981.

16. Vetter, L. Sugar and Spice Is Not the Answer. A Parent Handbook on the Career Implications of Sex Stereotyping. Columbus, Ohio: Ohio State University, Center for Vocational Education, 1977.

17. Walters, N. Parents: Key People to Assist in Occupational Decision Making. Jefferson City, Missouri: Missouri State Department of Education, 1974.

18. Werts, C. Parental Influence on Career Choice. Evanston, Illinois: National Merit Scholarship Corporation, 1967.

Part 2

Gender-Fair Teaching Competencies

Unit One

Competency

Develop an awareness of the effects of gender bias.

Performance Objective

Given a list of effects generated by the five class activities listed below, you will write a brief essay describing five limiting effects of gender bias on society and/or individuals. The essay should include the five effects identified through the class activities and the supporting rationale for each effect.

Learning Activities

Prerequisite: none

Activity 1. Read "Gender Bias in Schools," page 3.

Activity 2. Through small-group and class discussion, develop a questionnaire for use in Activity 3 to interview adults for the effects of gender bias in their lives. Possibilities for inclusion:

1. What types of activities (extracurricular, recreational, community, or home) were you encouraged to participate in by your parents, teachers, or counselors when you were in elementary and high school? Do you think this was because of your sex?
2. What types of courses were you encouraged to take or discouraged from taking by your parents, teachers, or counselors? Why?

3. What was your view of appropriate occupations for women and men when you were in high school? How did you form those opinions? Have your opinions changed?
4. What occupations did you consider as a child or young adult? Did you receive encouragement or discouragement from your parents, teachers, counselors, or other adults in your life? What was the outcome of others' influence on your occupational interests?
5. To what extent do you feel others had certain expectations of you because of your sex? Explain.

Activity 3. Obtain information on the effects of gender bias interviewing two men and two women using the questionnaire developed in Activity 2. (Class members could interview each other.)

Activity 4. Examine findings from interviews in small groups. Look for common themes and experiences. Identify positive and negative effects on the individuals and on society as a result of gender bias.

Activity 5. List the ten most common effects of gender bias identified in the interviews.

Evaluation

Write a brief essay outlining five limiting effects of gender bias on society and/or individuals. Your essay must include the effects identified through the class activities and the reading assignment. Provide supporting rationale for each effect.

Unit Two

Competency

Identify personal gender biases.

Performance Objective

In a discussion-group setting you will each identify a personal gender bias and describe its influence on yourself and others.

Learning Activities

Prerequisite: none

Activity 1. Complete "Questions about Women" on page 140 and "Questions About Men" on page 142 prior to completing Activity 2.

Activity 2. Read "Sexism in Education," page 19.

Activity 3. Discuss your responses to Activity 1 in small groups. Did the responses indicate gender bias? How might these biases influence yourself or others?

Activity 4. Read and discuss "How Fair Is Your Language?", page 58.

Activity 5. Complete the "Expectations Exercise." Discuss in small groups the "should" messages that were gender biased. Did these messages inhibit (or do they still inhibit) your career development? Discuss how these messages may have been an asset to your career development. Report your group discussion to the class.

Activity 6. Describe recent incidents in which you or others have done or said something that could be interpreted as exhibiting gender bias. Discuss in small groups the incidents, how you felt about them at the time, and what effect or influences they might have had on others. Report the concensus of your small group to the larger group or class.

Evaluation

Participate in the group discussions by identifying and sharing at least one personal gender bias and describing its influence.

Questions about Women

T	F		Questions
__	__	1.	A woman's primary role in life is raising children and taking care of her husband. Any career she has should fit around those responsibilities.
__	__	2.	A woman should work only if her husband cannot support her, if she has no children, or if she is single.
__	__	3.	Women make better elementary-school teachers than men.
__	__	4.	A woman who appears intelligent, aggressive, and demanding will probably have trouble finding a husband.
__	__	5.	Girls who engage in competitive sports run the risk of becoming muscular and unfeminine.
__	__	6.	Unattractive women are more in need of job skills than attractive women.

T	F		Questions
__	__	7.	A girl should never play better tennis than her boyfriend because it is bad for his ego.
__	__	8.	Men convey the authority and leadership necessary for school administration better than women do.
__	__	9.	Tomboyish behavior is unbecoming in a teenage girl.
__	__	10.	Women do not inspire confidence as brain surgeons, criminal lawyers, corporate executives, or military commanders.
__	__	11.	The fact that there have been so few women political leaders, artists, explorers, and scientists indicates that they do not have creative and intellectual ability.
__	__	12.	A man should stand when a women enters a room, give a woman his seat in a crowded bus, and hold the door open for a woman to enter first.
__	__	13.	It is more unbecoming for a woman to be intoxicated than for a man.
__	__	14.	There are still many jobs in which men should be given preference over women in hiring and promotion.
__	__	15.	Menstruating women should not engage in strenuous physical activity or in important decision making.
__	__	16.	While men can be expected to tell dirty jokes occasionally, women should never do so.
__	__	17.	A woman will never be truly satisfied unless she has been a wife and a mother.

T	F		Questions
__	__	18.	If a family has limited finances, it is more important to send a son to college than to send a daughter.
__	__	19.	There are some jobs that will never be suitable for women, such as automobile repair, bricklaying, and long-distance trucking.
__	__	20.	In the ideal family, the father works and the mother stays home and raises the children.

Questions about Men

T	F		Questions
__	__	1.	A man's primary responsibility in life is to support his family.
__	__	2.	To be respected, a man should be strong and self-reliant at all times.
__	__	3.	Physical strength and athletic prowess are the essence of masculinity.
__	__	4.	It is inappropriate for a man to show fear.
__	__	5.	It is embarrassing to see a male nurse, secretary, or flight attendant.
__	__	6.	Most men are too rough and insensitive to work with young children.
__	__	7.	A man who maintains the home and cares for his children while his wife works probably feels inadequate.

T	F		Questions
__	__	8.	In order to survive in a cutthroat world a man must be competitive and ambitious.
__	__	9.	It is more appropriate for a man to engage in extramarital affairs than for a woman.
__	__	10.	A man will never be truly satisfied unless he has been a husband and a father.
__	__	11.	A male elementary teacher is probably preparing himself to become a principal.
__	__	12.	Women are not attracted to yielding, sensitive, and unambitious men.
__	__	13.	Boys should be discouraged from choosing careers in dancing to avoid ridicule.
__	__	14.	Little boys should not be given dolls to play with unless they are masculine adventure dolls.
__	__	15.	A man should not marry a woman smarter than he is.
__	__	16.	It would be inappropriate for a business executive to have a male secretary.
__	__	17.	There is nothing wrong with a male college student expecting his girlfriend to type his papers, do his laundry, or cook for him if he reciprocates by taking her out.
__	__	18.	A man should not expect his date to pay for her own dinner.
__	__	19.	After dealing with the stress and pressure of the workplace all day, a man has the right to expect his wife to cater to him when he comes home.
__	__	20.	A man's life must revolve around his work first and his family second.

Expectations Exercise

In planning your career, you dealt with the expectations you placed on yourself and others placed on you. This exercise will help you become aware of these expectations. List each expectation and its source in the first column (e.g., I need a career that will support a family--father). Note whether the expectation ("should" message) was internal (came from yourself) or external (came from someone else) or both in the second and third columns. Then decide if the message indicated gender bias in the fourth column.

Expectation and Source ("should" messages)	Internal	External	Gender bias evident? Yes	No

Adapted from Born Free, Dr. L. Sunny Hansen, Project Director, WEEA Publishing Center, 1980.

Unit Three

Competency

Use gender-fair verbal interaction with students.

Performance Objective

Given the data gathered during the classroom observations and a role-playing situation, you will identify and use gender-fair verbal interaction with male and female students. The types and kinds of interaction with male and female students will be balanced according to the "Checklist for Verbal Interaction."

Learning Activities

Prerequisite: none

Activity 1. Read "Between Teacher and Student," page 66.

Activity 2. Do the exercise "How Sexist Am I as a Teacher?", page 146.

Activity 3. Share "best" and "worst" personal experiences with gender-fair and gender-unfair teachers. In a small group discussion, list examples, and select group recorders to report examples to the entire class.

Activity 4. Role play or read the "Gender-Fair Verbal Interaction Script" on page 148. Use the "Checklist for Verbal Interaction" to record the kinds of teacher interaction with students. Discuss in class.

Activity 5. Observe actual teacher-student interaction (if possible) using the "Observation Sheet for Verbal Interaction Assessment" on page 150 to record the frequencies and kinds of teacher interaction with students. Prepare an analysis of the data gathered which includes answers to the following questions.

1. Does the teacher exhibit gender-fair verbal interaction?
2. How is this behavior exhibited?
3. How often does the teacher exhibit this behavior?
4. What suggestions can you make to improve behavior?

Report your findings back to the class.

Evaluation

In a role-playing situation, demonstrate gender-fair verbal interaction with students and identify these behaviors in others using the "Checklist for Verbal Interaction", page 151.

How Sexist Am I as a Teacher?

Yes	No	
__	__	Do I generally praise a male student for being big and strong?
__	__	Do I pity girls who are unable or unwilling to be "fashionable"?
__	__	Do I ever say that girls should wear dresses?
__	__	Do I ask girls to do the housework-type tasks?

Yes	No	
___	___	Do I ask boys to do the executive duties or heavy work?
___	___	Do I pity boys who are unable or unwilling to engage in competitive sports?
___	___	Do I call special attention to those who are athletic?
___	___	Do I ever say about a girl, she acts so boyish?
___	___	Do I find myself using a different tone of voice with a boy than a girl?
___	___	Do I ever discourage a girl from going into a career in which there are few women?
___	___	Do I ever tease a boy for being a "sissy"?
___	___	Do I notice when there are more sports activities for boys than for girls?
___	___	Do I react when I find that there are limited activities for boys in art, drama, and dance?
___	___	Do I segregate boys and girls for any activity?
___	___	Do I ever say "Now boys and girls" rather than "students" or "now class"?
___	___	Do I invite more male role models than female role models for class speakers?
___	___	Do I use slang terms such as "fag," "tomboy," or "chick"?
___	___	Do I expect girls to do the decorating at a party?

Yes	No	
__	__	Do I believe that a girl's first priority is to plan for marriage and childbearing?
__	__	Do I find myself encouraging more boys to go to college than girls?
__	__	Do I expect more scholarships to go to boys than to girls?
__	__	Do I expect boys to be more mathematical than girls?
__	__	When a girl says that she is not very good in math, do I reply that most girls aren't?
__	__	Do I tend to discipline girls more leniently than boys?
__	__	Would I encourage a young pregnant high school woman to remain in the regular school program?

Gender-Fair Verbal Interaction Script

Teacher: All right boys and girls, let's review your homework. Please put your papers on your desks.

Teacher: Amy, this is very neat.

Teacher: Sue, what is the answer to question three?

Teacher: Yes, that is correct. Joe, do you have the same answer? Please explain to the class how you arrived at that answer.

Teacher: Dave, you have a good answer for question one but question two is weak. I would like you to redo question two during recess.

Teacher: Let's review some of yesterday's lesson. Ralph, Sam, Lorna, and Debbie, please go to the board.

The teacher places a math problem on the board before each student and instructs the students to complete the problem.

Teacher: My you finished quickly, Sam. You did such a good job. Here, try this problem. It is a little more difficult.

Teacher: Lorna, you made an error at the very beginning. You seem to be unable to do this kind of problem.

The teacher shows Lorna where the error is and waits while Lorna refigures that part of the problem.

Teacher: OK, Debbie, you may sit down.

Teacher: Ralph, look closely at your solution. I know you can do better if you will think.

Ralph studies his solution and quickly realizes that he has misplaced a decimal point. He makes the correction.

Teacher: It is always important to check your work carefully, Ralph. Do not hurry with math.

See Answer Key on page 153.

Observation Sheet for Verbal Interaction Assessment

Directions

For each category indicated, tally the teacher comments directed at boys and girls. Refer to the definition of each category if necessary (see page 89).

	Teachers Comments Directed at:			
	Boys	Total	Girls	Total
I. Praise				
A. Academic	____	____	____	____
B. Nonacademic	____	____	____	____
II. Academic Criticism				
A. Intellectual quality	____	____	____	____
B. Effort	____	____	____	____
III. Nonacademic Criticism				
A. Mild	____	____	____	____
B. Harsh	____	____	____	____
IV. Questions				
A. Low level	____	____	____	____
B. High level	____	____	____	____
V. Academic Intervention				
A. Facilitative	____	____	____	____
B. Disruptive	____	____	____	____

Checklist for Verbal Interaction

	Frequently	Sometimes	Never
1. Using the data gathered on the chart:			
a. Does the teacher praise girls and boys equitably for the intellectual quality of their written and verbal work?	______	______	______

Examples and comments:

	Frequently	Sometimes	Never
b. Does the teacher praise boys and girls equitably for the appearance, form, and neatness of their written work?	______	______	______

Examples and comments:

	Frequently	Sometimes	Never
c. Does the teacher criticize girls and boys equitably for the intellectual quality of their written and verbal work?	______	______	______

Examples and comments:

	Frequently	Sometimes	Never
d. Does the teacher criticize boys and girls equitably for written work that fails to meet standards for form, neatness, and appearance?	______	______	______

Examples and comments:

	Frequently	Sometimes	Never
2. Does the teacher encourage both girls and boys to try harder so they will be more likely to attribute failure to insufficient effort rather than to lack of ability?	______	______	______

Examples and comments:

	Frequently	Sometimes	Never
a. Does the teacher ask knowledge-level questions of boys and girls equitably?	______	______	______
b. Does the teacher ask evaluation- and application-level questions of boys and girls equitably?	______	______	______

Answer Key
Gender-Fair Verbal Interaction

Teacher: All right boys and girls,(1) let's review your homework. Please put your papers on your desks.

Teacher: Amy, this is very neat.(2)

Teacher: Sue, what is the answer(3) to question three?

Teacher: Yes(4), that is correct. Joe, do you have the same answer? Please explain(5) to the class how you arrived at that answer.

Teacher: Dave, you have a good answer for question one but question two is weak. I would like you to redo(6) question two during recess.

Teacher: Let's review some of yesterday's lesson. Ralph, Sam, Lorna, and Debbie, please go to the board.

The teacher places a math problem on the board before each student and instructs the students to complete the problem.

Teacher: My you finished quickly, Sam. You did such a good job.(7) Here, try this problem. It is a little more difficult.(8)

Teacher: Lorna, you made an error at the very beginning. You seem to be unable(9) to do this kind of problem.

The teacher shows Lorna(10) where the error is and waits while Lorna refigures that part of the problem.

Teacher: OK,(11) Debbie, you may sit down.

Teacher: Ralph, look closely(12) at your solution. I know you can do better(13) if you will think.

Ralph studies his solution and quickly realizes that he has misplaced a decimal point. He makes the correction.

Teacher: It is always important to check your work carefully, Ralph.(14) Do not hurry with math.

See page 89 for detailed descriptions of categories.

1. Reference to sex is not necessary (students)
2. Nonacademic praise of female
3. Low-level question to female
4. Acceptance but no praise for academic accomplishment of female
5. High-level question to male
6. Harsh criticism/punishment of male
7. Academic praise of male
8. High-level task for male
9. Criticism of intellectual ability of female
10. Disruptive academic intervention for female
11. Acceptance but no praise for academic accomplishment of female
12. Facilitative academic intervention for male
13. Academic criticism of effort rather than of intellectual quality for male
14. Mild nonacademic criticism of male.

Unit Four

Competency

Use gender-fair nonverbal interaction with students.

Performance Objective

Given a simulated teaching situation you will identify and use gender-fair nonverbal behaviors that support improved teacher-student communication and classroom management using at least three behaviors from the "Nonverbal Behaviors Checklist" marked "frequently" and no behavior marked "never."

Learning Activities

Prerequisite: read "Gender Bias in Schools," page 3 and "Sexism in Education," page 19.

Activity 1. Read "Gender-Fair Nonverbal Behaviors," page 156.

Activity 2. Read "Nonverbal Behaviors Script," page 156.

Activity 3. Observe a class (preferably a job-oriented class) with both males and females. Using the "Evaluation Sheet: Focus on Nonverbal Interaction" on page 161, identify nonverbal behaviors. Report findings to the class.

Activity 4. In small groups, develop a plan for eliminating gender-biased nonverbal behaviors.

Evaluation

In a simulated teaching situation evaluate each other's nonverbal behaviors using the "Nonverbal Behaviors Checklist," on page 162.

Gender-Fair Nonverbal Behaviors

Overcoming Gender Bias in Nonverbal Teaching Behaviors

The eyes are very important when establishing relationships between the teacher and students. Take care to use them with discretion. For example, a wink can communicate, I notice what you are doing, or it can be received as, I think you are special and would like to see you privately. The latter meaning must be avoided. You should take care to establish eye contact with all members of the class. Maintain contact until a student has finished talking to you.

Circulate around the room, positioning yourself in different areas to influence the degree of involvement of both boys and girls in learning.

Make a conscious effort to encourage equal participation among all students by using nonverbal reinforcement behaviors such as leaning toward students to listen more carefully, moving closer, nodding affirmatively, smiling, and using appropriate physical contact such as a hand shake.

Make sure you are using the same amount of "wait time" so that both boys and girls have an opportunity to formulate a response to your question or to finish a particular task.

When seating or formulating groups of students, use categories other than gender to divide the class.

Nonverbal Behaviors Script

Directions

The following is a description of Mr. Best's ninth-grade general business class. Make note of his nonverbal behavior. Mr. Best has been teaching for several years and is well liked by students, parents, and other teachers.

Mr. Best: Good morning!

Mr. Best looks around the room to see who is absent.

Lori: Mr. Best, I have a question about last night's assignment.

While Mr. Best continues to record the attendance, he glances up and nods.

Mr. Best: Yes?

Lori: You asked us to find examples of promotion sales and clearance sales, but I'm not clear on the difference.

Mr. Best: George, can you explain the difference to Lori?

After several seconds have gone by with no response, Mr. Best tries again.

Mr. Best: Sue, can you tell us the difference?

Sue hesitates a moment and looks down at her book. Mr. Best rolls his eyes toward the ceiling and begins to explain the difference himself. Mr. Best begins the day's lesson, Being an Informed Consumer; he asks frequent questions during his lecture.

Mr. Best: Betty, tell us what services the Better Business Bureau offers.

As Betty gives her answer, Mr. Best walks to the window and watches a physical education class play baseball.

Mr. Best: Thanks, Betty, that was a very thorough overview of their services.

Mr. Best walks over to the rear of the room and stands behind Dick.

Mr. Best: Dick, do you know where the local Better Business Bureau is located?

Dick shrugs and shakes his head indicating that he does not.

Mr. Best: Come on now, Dick, you have lived in this town all of your life.

Mr. Best looks to Joe sitting across from Dick.

Mr. Best: Well, Joe, how could Dick find out where the bureau is located?

Joe: The telephone directory? Have you ever reported a company to the Better Business Bureau?

Mr. Best: Yes, I have.

Mr. Best moves to the front of the room and tells the class about a problem he had the previous year with a local auto repair firm.

Sandra: Mr. Best, my mother had the same problem with that company.

Mr. Best nods his head and calls on Tom who has raised his hand.

Tom: So did my brother!

Mr. Best looks at Tom and Tom continues with the story of his brother's problem with the repair company.

Mr. Best: Knowing where to report a company and where to get reliable information is only one aspect of being an informed consumer. You also have to know how to make decisions.

Looking at Sam, Mr. Best asks him to tell the class about his last major purchase. Sam relates that he had to help his older sister locate and buy a car stereo. Mr. Best nods and asks him to list all of the decisions he and his sister made regarding the purchase. He continues to look at Sam and nods occasionally to encourage Sam to continue.

Mr. Best: Beth, how about you? Have you made any purchases lately?

Beth, never at a loss for words, begins to talk about her latest shopping trip with her parents to look for a new television. As she relates the story, Mr. Best begins to pass out a sheet of paper. When Beth finishes, he thanks her for her input.

Mr. Best: Now, let's have a contest. All the boys move to the right side of the room, and all the girls to the left.

The students move as directed. They have done this type of exercise before and are looking forward to another of Mr. Best's games.

Mr. Best: Let's find out who the better shoppers are, boys or girls. I have just given each of you a list of products and some information about each product, including the price. I am going to give each group the same amount of money and a shopping list; you make decisions about which products should be selected. You will have fifteen minutes to make your selections. You may not go over the amount of money specified, and each item on your list or a substitution must be purchased. Linda, please pass out the shopping list. One to each student.

The students ask a few questions to be sure they understand the rules, and they quickly begin to work to prove they are the best shoppers. Mr. Best walks around the room and monitors the progress being made by the two groups. He looks over the girls' list and nods approvingly. When he reaches the boys' group, he sits down and listens to their reasoning on one item. He does not offer an opinion, but lets them

come to their own conclusion. At the end of fifteen minutes, Mr. Best interrupts the student and collects their shopping lists and their purchases. Mr. Best then sits down at his desk in front of the classroom.

Mr. Best: Candy, what problems did your group run into?

Candy hesitates. Mr. Best studies the girls' lists.

Mr. Best: Joyce, do you recall any examples of group disagreement about the choice of a purchase?

When Joyce finishes, he tells them he thinks they made the right choices.

Mr. Best: Martin, I heard you explaining to Steve why a lower-priced item may not necessarily be of lesser quality. Why do you feel this is true?

Martin: I don't know; I guess my dad told me.

Mr. Best leans forward in his chair and looks at Martin, waiting for him to continue. Martin pauses for a few seconds and then continues with an explanation about how his father's company can undersell a competitor even though the product quality is very similar.

Mr. Best: Class time is about over for today. Steve and Joe, please realign the desks in straight rows. Candy, you are in charge of collecting last night's homework.

See Answer Key on page 163.

Evaluation Sheet: Focus on Nonverbal Behavior

Directions

During a teaching episode, record nonverbal behaviors that effect classroom climate. Look for the five nonverbal behaviors in the left-hand column. Then record examples of each in the middle column and indicate whether the behavior is sex-fair or sex-biased in the right-hand column.

Nonverbal Behaviors	Examples	Gender-Fair	Biased
1. Eye contact			
2. Positioning of teacher with respect to students			
3. Use of reinforcement behavior (leaning toward students, moving closer, etc.)			
4. Wait time			
5a. Integration of students into gender-fair seating and group work			
5b. Assignment of tasks equally distributed (carrying books, doing math, running machines, collecting lunch money, putting away materials)			

Nonverbal Behavior Checklist

Directions

Record each example of the gender-fair behaviors and their frequencies.

Behavior	Example	Frequently	Sometimes	Never
Eye contact				
Position				
Reinforcement				
Wait time				
Groups/Tasks				

Gender-Fair Answer Key
Nonverbal Behaviors Script

Directions

The following is a description of Mr. Best's ninth-grade general business class. Make note of his nonverbal behavior. Mr. Best has been teaching for several years and is well liked by students, parents, and other teachers.

Mr. Best: Good morning!

Mr. Best looks around the room to see who is absent.

Lori: Mr. Best, I have a question about last night's assignment.

While Mr. Best continues to record (1) the attendance, he glances up and nods.

Mr. Best: Yes?

Lori: You asked us to find examples of promotion sales and clearance sales, but I'm not clear on the difference.

Mr. Best: George, can you explain the difference to Lori?

After several seconds have gone by with no response, Mr. Best tries again.

Mr. Best: Sue, can you tell us the difference?

Sue hesitates a moment (2) and looks down at her book. Mr. Best rolls his eyes toward the ceiling and begins to explain the difference himself. Mr. Best begins the day's lesson, Being an Informed Consumer; he asks frequent questions during his lecture.

Mr. Best: Betty, tell us what services the Better Business Bureau offers.

As Betty gives her answer, Mr. Best walks to the window and watches (3) a physical education class play baseball.

Mr. Best: Thanks, Betty, that was a very thorough overview of their services.

Mr. Best walks over to the rear of the room and stands behind Dick (4).

Mr. Best: Dick, do you know where the local Better Business Bureau is located?

Dick shrugs and shakes his head indicating that he does not.

Mr. Best: Come on now, Dick, you have lived in this town all of your life.

Mr. Best looks to Joe (5) sitting across from Dick.

Mr. Best: Well, Joe, how could Dick find out where the bureau is located?

Joe: The telephone directory? Have you ever reported a company to the Better Business Bureau?

Mr. Best: Yes, I have.

Mr. Best moves to the front of the room and tells the class about a problem he had the previous year with a local auto repair firm.

Sandra: Mr. Best, my mother had the same problem with that company.

Mr. Best nods his head and calls on Tom (6) who has raised his hand.

Tom: So did my brother!

Mr. Best looks at Tom (7) and Tom continues with the story of his brother's problem with the repair company.

Mr. Best: Knowing where to report a company and where to get reliable information is only one aspect of being an informed consumer. You also have to know how to make decisions.

Looking at Sam (8), Mr. Best asks him to tell the class about his last major purchase. Sam relates that he had to help his older sister locate and buy a car stereo. Mr. Best nods and asks (9) him to list all of the decisions he and his sister made regarding the purchase. He continues to look at Sam and nods occasionally (10) to encourage Sam to continue.

Mr. Best: Beth, how about you? Have you made any purchases lately?

Beth, never at a loss for words, beings to talk about her latest shopping trip with her parents to look for a new television. As she relates the story, Mr. Best begins to pass out a sheet of paper(11). When Beth finishes, he thanks her for her input.

Mr. Best: Now, let's have a contest. All the boys move to the right side of the room, and all the girls to the left(12).

The students move as directed. They have done this type of exercise before and are looking forward to another of Mr. Best's games.

Mr. Best: Let's find out who the better shoppers are, boys or girls(13). I have just given each of you a list of products and some information about each product, including the price. I am going to give each group the same amount of money and a shopping list; you make decisions about which products should be selected. You will have fifteen minutes to make your selections. You may not go over the amount of money specified, and each item on your list or a substitution must be purchased. Linda, please pass out the shopping list(14). One to each student.

The students ask a few questions to be sure they understand the rules, and they quickly begin to work to prove they are the best shoppers. Mr. Best walks around the room and monitors the progress being made by the two groups. He looks over the girls' list and nods approvingly. When he reaches the boys' group, he sits down and listens to their reasoning (15) on one item. He does not offer an opinion, but lets them come to their own conclusion. At the end of fifteen minutes, Mr. Best interrupts the student and collects their shopping lists and their purchases. Mr. Best then sits down at his desk in front of the classroom.

Mr. Best: Candy, what problems did your group run into?

Candy hesitates(16). Mr. Best studies the girls' lists.

Mr. Best: Joyce, do you recall any examples of group disagreement about the choice of a purchase?

When Joyce finishes, he tells them he thinks they made the right choices.

Mr. Best: Martin, I heard you explaining to Steve why a lower-priced item may not necessarily be of lesser quality. Why do you feel this is true?

Martin: I don't know; I guess my dad told me.

Mr. Best leans forward in his chair and looks at (17) Martin, waiting for him to continue. Martin pauses for a few seconds and then continues with an explanation about how his father's company can undersell a competitor even though the product quality is very similar.

Mr. Best: Class time is about over for today. Steve and Joe, please realign (18) the desks in straight rows. Candy, you are in charge of collecting last night's homework.

1. Does not maintain eye contact with female.
2. Brief wait time for female.
3. Does not maintain eye contact or close position with female.
4. Close position with male.
5. Attention from male to male.
6. Positive reinforcement of male.
7. Maintains eye contact with male.
8. Maintains eye contact with male.
9. Positive reinforcement of male.
10. Maintains eye contact and continues reinforcing male.
11. Does not maintain eye contact or use positive reinforcement with female.
12. Divides class by sex for no specific need.
13. Put males and females against each other.
14. Helping task for female.
15. Close position and attention to males.
16. Brief wait time for female.
17. Long wait time for male, close positioning and eye contact for male.
18. Tasks assigned by sex.

Unit Five

Competency

Identify gender-fair curriculum materials.

Performance Objective

Given a checklist and access to curriculum materials in your teaching area you will find examples of the six types of gender bias found in curriculum materials.

Learning Activities

Prerequisite: read "Gender Bias In Schools," page 3 and "Sexism in Education," page 19.

Activity 1. Read "Confronting Sex Bias in Instructional Materials," page 98.

Activity 2. Read the "Case Studies" on page 169 and identify the types of gender bias. (You may work in small groups.)

Activity 3. Brainstorm strategies for counteracting gender bias in curriculum materials.

Evaluation

Locate an example of each of the six types of gender bias frequently found in curriculum materials. Use the "Checklist for Evaluating Curriculum and Instructional Materials" on page 173 as a guide.

Case Studies

Directions

Read each excerpt and determine if gender bias is present. If you find bias, indicate which form is present. By the way, as is the case in so many textbooks, you may come across more than just one form of bias in each excerpt. Finally, assume the role of author and rewrite the excerpt so that bias is no longer reflected.

Case 1

The contemporary farmer is radically different from the frontiersman of the past. He is knowledgeable about this complex, scientific endeavor, and his livelihood is dependent upon his efficiency.

Is gender bias present?
What form of gender bias is present?
Suggested revision:

Case 2

In a mathematics workbook there are thirty-one word problems showing males and females involved in the following activities:

Boys	Girls
1. buying a model car	1. deciding whether to plant grass around a doghouse
2. painting (two times)	2. figuring out the living space

Selections are taken by permission from Sex Equity Handbook for Schools, Longman Inc. and from Building Sex Equity In Vocational Education, Illinois State Board of Education.

Boys	Girls
3. walking (four times)	3. working for her father
4. making a map	4. drinking
5. doing an experiment	5. working
6. making a paper chain	6. making a paper chain
7. losing weight	7. gaining weight
8. riding a bicycle	8. growing taller
9. running a race	9. missing questions
10. swimming	10. driving boys home
11. using calories (two times)	
12. driving a delivery truck	
13. buying land (two times)	

Is gender bias present?
What form of gender bias is present?
Suggested revision:

Case 3

Women were given the vote as a reward for their work in World War I.

Is gender bias present?
What form of gendeer bias is present?
Suggested revision:

Case 4

An architect must have a great deal of knowledge about materials and construction. He translates the ideas of his client into reality by ingenious planning and designing.

Is gender bias present?
What form of gender bias is present?
Suggested revision:

Case 5

The following is taken from an instructional unit on work and careers. The materials deals with ways students can explore careers and part-time jobs. Picture A has a boy walking three dogs with the following statement over it: "Taking care of pets may be a way of earning money." Picture B has a female in a candy-striper uniform with the following statement under it: "Survey the possibilities for doing vlounteer work in your community that would serve as a kind of work experience for you."

Is gender bias present?
What form of gender bias is present?
Suggested revision:

Case 6

The following is an excerpt from a section of a book in which suggestions are given to teachers for leading a discussion of graphic arts as a career. "Do any of you have an idea of what you'd like to do? You'll be working for more than 40 years after high school." The class moaned. "John, what subjects do you want to take while in high school?" ...When John has an idea of who he is and what he wants from a job, he is ready to explore career opportunities. He is going to make the career fit him." No examples are provided with female names. The importance of working with females on career exploration is never mentioned.

Is gender bias present?
What form of gender bias is present?
Suggested revision:

Case 7

A recruitment brochure from a secretarial school shows a picture of two women sitting in an office at typewriters and three men standing in the foreground wearing business suits. The following caption is given: "Not all who work for the construction industry are found at the project site. Secretaries and receptionists work in office buildings and receive their training outside the industry."

Is gender bias present?
What form of gender bias is present?
Suggested revision:

Case 8

Unit on "Care of the Body" shows only pictures of girls taking care of their hair and clothes.

Is gender bias present?
What form of gender bias is present?
Suggested revision:

See Answer Key on page 174.

Checklist for Evaluating Curriculum and Instructional Materials

Directions

Use the following evaluation tool to determine whether the curriculum and instruction materials are gender fair. Comments may include page references, descriptions, or recommendations for improvement.

	Yes	No	Comments
1. Does the textbook make a special effort to include pictures of male and female students in nontraditional roles?	___	___	________
2. Do curriculum materials make both female and male students feel comfortable in learning about the subject?	___	___	________
3. Do learning activities and projects avoid sex-role stereotyping according to past traditional roles?	___	___	________
4. Are the accomplishments of both sexes included in the text?	___	___	________
5. Does the textbook point out to both males and females the opportunities that will be available to them upon completion of this vocational program?	___	___	________

	Yes	No	Comments
6. Do the textbook and the other curriculum materials dispel the myth that equipment and machinery are more appropriate for males?	___	___	___
7. Are the learning activities equal in their distribution of exciting role models for both boys and girls?	___	___	___
8. Does the textbook or course title reflect generic terms such as "Living Single" rather than a title like "Bachelor Living?"	___	___	___

Answer Key to Case Studies

Case 1
Is gender bias present? Yes
What form of gender bias is present? Linguistic, Invisibility, and Stereotyping

Suggested revision. Male and female farmers should both be referred to. The use of the pronoun he to refer to all farmers should be revised. The use of frontiersman is an example of sexist language and serves to deny the contributions and experiences of pioneering women. This noun should be replaced with pioneers, frontier settlers, or pioneering men and women.

Case 2
Is gender bias present? Yes
What form of gender bias is present? Stereotyping and Invisibility

Suggested revision. More than twice as many males as females appear in these thirty-one word problems--a characteristic of invisibility. Males are more active and participate in "more important" activities than females. Revisions should include females participating in an equitable number of active and important roles.

Case 3
Is gender bias present? Yes
What form of gender bias is present? Imbalance and Selectivity, and Linguistic

Suggested revision. This neglects the seventy-years' struggle by women for the right to vote. The physical abuse and sacrifices suffered by leaders and participants in the struggle are negated by this oversimplification. The sentence might be rewritten to read, "Over seventy years after the Seneca Falls Convention, women won the right to vote."

Case 4
Is gender bias present? Yes
What form of gender bias is present? Linguistic

Suggested revision. The use of "he" to refer to all architects should be revised. Both male and female architects should be referred to. A suggested revision might read, "Architects translate the ideas of their clients into reality by ingenious planning and design."

Case 5
Is gender bias present? Yes
What form of gender bias is present? Stereotyping and Unreality

Suggested revision. These pictures suggest the stereotype that boys work with animals and females serve in health occupations. It also suggests that men work for pay and women do volunteer work. A revision might include illustrations of both boys and girls working for pay and doing volunteer work.

Case 6
Is gender bias present? Yes
What form of gender bias is present? Invisibility and Unreality

Suggested revision. The selection suggests that only males should be planning for a career. A revision should make the point that both females and males should prepare for careers. A revision would suggest, "Maria, what subjects do you want to take in high school? It is important that you plan for a career that fits you."

Case 7
Is gender bias present? Yes
What form of gender bias is present? Exclusion and Stereotyping and Isolation

Suggested revision. The portrayal of women as secretaries who are assuming background roles perpetuates stereotyping and isolation. The portrayal of men in the foreground of the picture further suggests a subordinate role for women. It should be revised by including pictures of women in a variety of roles with a caption such as "Secretaries and receptionists work in a variety of settings and may use their secretarial experience to move into many career areas."

Case 8
Is gender bias present? Yes
What form of gender bias is present? Invisibility, Stereotyping, and Unreality

Suggested revision. This unit reflects the stereotype that only girls are interested in grooming. Because there are no pictures of boys taking care of their clothes or hair, they are invisible and a reality of daily life for all persons is omitted. A revision should include information about grooming that applies both to boys and girls.

Unit Six

Competency

Encourage students to broaden their occupational choices.

Performance Objective

Given your teaching specialty, plan several activities that will provide students with multiple gender-fair occupational options.

Learning Activities

Prerequisites: none

Activity 1. Read "Occupational Options," page 178.

Activity 2. In small groups discuss the trends and information provided in the reading from Activity 1. Generate additional suggestions on how educators can broaden occupational choices for students.

Activity 3. Review the examples of "Expanding Options" on page 179. Look for gender bias and make suggestions for gender-fair revision.

Activity 4. Plan activities to broaden occupational choices and insert these activities onto the "Occupational Information Calendar" on page 183. Note the calendar has one activity already planned. This activity has also been evaluated on the "Evaluation Checklist" on page 184. Insert the activites you have planned onto the calendar. Evaluate each activity with the activity evaluation guide. Provide a brief description of each activity and the amount of time each activity will need. Include any resources that must be obtained for use with the activities. Include an estimate of all costs associated with the activities.*

Evaluation

The planned activities will meet all items on the "Evaluation Checklist," page 184.

Occupational Options

One barrier students face in planning their futures is the limitations they have put on themselves. These self-imposed limitations are too often tied to gender. Traditional ideas about which roles are appropriate for men and women in the workplace can limit a student's dreams and expectations. Young men may believe that they have to behave in certain ways to be "masculine," such as being interested in mechanical or analytical vocations rather than in the arts and social sciences and being emotionally in control as opposed to being sensitive or vulnerable. Stereotyped role expectations for young women include choosing the so-called helping professions (teaching, nursing, social work) over other vocations, being nurturing and considerate of others' feelings while ignoring their own needs, or submitting to the preferences and demands of a male partner in a personal or work relationship.

---

*Occupational information, including ten-to-twenty-year employment projections, salary ranges, educational requirements, and working conditions, can be found in publications such as the Occupational Outlook Handbook and the Guide for Occupational Exploration. Both resources are published by the U.S. Department of Labor.

Adapted from Male or Female: Is My Life Already Planned? Life-Planning Education, Washington, D.C. March 1985.

Stereotyped thinking is learned very early and is difficult to overcome. Many youths will pattern their behavior and shape their future plans to be consistent with traditional sex-role expectations. If these young people are to overcome stereotyped attitudes about what their adult roles are to be, they must recognize that traditional patterns are changing and that they can take on nontraditional jobs, careers, and family roles. For example, a man can play a major role in caring for children and a woman can learn to make home repairs. And women and men can pursue vocations once considered only appropriate for the other sex.

Young women, especially, must deal with the fact that there are few role models for them to look up to. Though the 1980s have seen for the first time a woman on the Supreme Court, a woman in space, and a woman nominated for national office by a major party, these instances have been isolated and treated as extraordinary events by the media. Only when the presence of women in such occupations is commonplace will young women know that they can strive for the jobs once considered "men's" positions.

Long-standing social attitudes can be difficult to change. Young people will need help to see that new options are possible; they will need support from adults and peers if they pursue nontraditional paths.

Expanding Options*

Encourage all students to make academic, career, and personal decisions on the basis of individual abilities, interests, and values rather than on the basis of gender.

Encourage students to pursue a career even though the people in that field are primarily of the other sex.

Use nontraditional role models--men and women for career-day guests, as mentors, and in classroom instruction.

Discuss job salaries with male and female students.

---

*Adapted from Voice, a quarterly publication of the New York State Sex Equity Technical Assistance and Resource Center.

Point out that typically female jobs mean lower salaries than typically male jobs.

Discuss armed-services opportunities with male and female students.

Meet with nontraditional students on a regular basis to support them in their pioneering roles and to discuss any problems that may arise.

Provide students about to enter the work force with information about their employment rights and current discrimination laws.

Special Help for Boys and Young Men

Encourage a wide range of job options, including traditionally female occupations, even if they have already made a tentative career decision.

Help them understand the changing roles of men and women and the effects this may have on their work and family lives.

Arrange discussion groups and speakers for the topic socialization pressures on males.

Remind male students about household- and family-maintenance courses when arranging schedules. Most of them will need to be prepared for an active role in home and family life.

Special Help for Girls and Young Women

Encourage a wide range of job options, including traditionally male occupations, even if they have already made a tentative career decision.

Provide realistic information about their probable job futures. Most girls can expect to have paying jobs even if they marry and have families.

Recognize barriers that young women raise for themselves in response to socialization pressures.

Encourage college-bound girls to take three or four years of math when arranging schedules. Remind girls about the availability of industrial-arts and physical-education courses.

Schedule discussion groups for girls about mutual problems and future alternatives.

Use of Materials

Review all counseling and testing materials for sources of sex bias, and modify where appropriate.

Find materials that use nonsexist pronouns and depict both traditional and nontraditional jobs.

Find materials that mention the changing roles of women and men in our society.

Place your name (and your colleagues') on the mailing lists of companies and groups developing nonracist and nonsexist materials.

Discontinue use of vocational preference tests with separate forms for females and males.

Write publishers of standardized tests about the sexual and racial biases in the contents of test items.

Encourage a districtwide review of counseling materials that might be reinforcing biases and stereotypes.

Point out stereotyped males and females in career materials.

Coordinate bulletin boards and displays portraying pictures of women and men working at a variety of jobs, including nontraditional jobs.

Nonacademic Guidance

For both boys and girls encourage leadership. Encourage them to join clubs and groups traditionally dominated by the other sex.

Emphasize the importance of athletic experiences and have them actively seek athletic scholarships.

Contact with Parents

Try to develop closer school contacts with fathers as well as mothers.

Whenever possible, work to dispel myths about single parents and their families.

Point out expanding options to parents as well as students. Attempt to educate parents on an on-going basis about the need for expanded career options and the need to prepare their children for both home and work realities.

Provide teachers in appropriate subject areas with information that can be incorporated into classes on changing patterns of work and family life.

When presented with a situation in which a student's options are limited by a staff member's actions, take steps to intervene.

Develop administrative and peer support to identify situations involving gender bias.

Equity Advocate on Staff

Encourage your district to provide new and earlier opportunities for students to explore nontraditional options at elementary and junior-high levels.

Meet with teachers of nontraditional students to discuss the importance of their role in recruitment and retention.

Remind key people that changes in today's work force make it necessary to expand nontraditional options.

Review economic, social, and demographic trends that may affect student career and life choices.

Publicize information about work force trends to colleagues.

A positive role model is the best counselor. School personnel who consistently act and speak in an equitable manner offer invaluable guidance to students.

Occupational Information Calendar

Directions

For each activity listed on the calendar, provide a brief explanation of that activity. Note the bulletin board example.

September	October	November	December
Monthly bulletin board			

January	February	March	April	May

Brief Explanation of Each Activity

Activity 1: Bulletin Board

A section of the classroom bulletin board will be designated "Career Opportunities" and will present information about specific careers. A different career will be shown every month. The instructor will organize the first bulletin board. Groups of students will be assigned to the following months. All materials must be current and gender fair. The cost will be minimal.

Evaluation Checklist

Directions

Use this checklist to evaluate your planned activities. Each activity is evaluated with the criteria listed in the left-hand column. Place a key word to identify each activity in the area labeled activities across the top of the column. Note, the bulletin-board example has been evaluated.

Occupational Information Activities

Criteria	Bulletin Board	Activities
Appropriate for age and education of student	X	
Provides occupational information not readily available to students	X	
Activity will be of interest to students	X	
Cost has been determined and is reasonable	X	
Resources are available	X	
Activity is gender fair	X	

Unit Seven

Competency

Plan activities to recruit and retain nontraditional students.

Performance Objective

Given a yearly planning calendar plan activities to recruit and retain nontraditional students. Each activity will be free of gender bias or subtle sex-role stereotyping.

Learning Activities

Prerequisite: none

Activity 1. Read "Who Should Recruit," page 186.

Activity 2. Review "Sample Recruitment Strategies," page 189.

Activity 3. Review "Sample Recruitment/Retention Calendar," page 192.

Activity 4. In small groups, brainstorm additional ideas for a recruitment/retention calendar.

Activity 5. Prepare a calendar of recruitment activities for a school year.

Activity 6. Use the "Calendar Checklist," page 193 to evaluate calendars developed by other groups in the class.

Evaluation

The calendar of activities and description of activities will meet at least seven of the eight criteria on the evaluation checklist.

Who Should Recruit?

Administrators, counselors, educators, or staff who are assigned responsibilities for recruitment must possess certain characteristics for success. Some of these characteristics:

1. The ability to fulfill a "counselor" role as interaction with all types of individuals occurs.

2. The ability to listen to, analyze, and synthesize information, and to provide available alternatives based on that information for a prospective student to consider.

3. A commitment to people and education.

4. The ability to realistically promote the overall benefits of education and the willingness to follow through immediately to help individuals.

5. A familiarity with labor needs and job requirements in a community.

6. A continuing relationship with various segments of the community (e.g., social agencies, service agencies, social groups, Chamber of Commerce).

Many research studies indicate that teachers have an important influence on female and male students in reinforcing their thinking about career decisions, encouraging them to think more broadly about their decisions,

---

Adapted from FAIR Recruitment, Model and Strategies, Department of Adult, Vocational and Technical Education/Illinois State Board of Education, 1980.

serving as role models, relating attitudes and information that affect students' self-esteem, distributing literature, and showing films that address the career decision-making process. The ideal situation probably finds teachers, guidance counselors, and administrators involved in a collaborative recruitment effort. While teachers may believe that career counseling is the proper domain of guidance counselors, nontraditional enrollment in education is not likely to increase unless teachers assume at least part of this function. No matter how much support counselors give students, they will not enroll without the assurance that teachers believe in nontraditional equity. Peers also make good recruiters. This will be effective at a later stage of the effort when enrolled nontraditional students are available to share their successful experiences and tips on overcoming problems.

Individuals selected for recruitment assignments must be committed to the principle that education is for all segments of the population including those people categorized by sex, age, handicap, and ethnic culture.

Recruiting Male and Female Students

The following suggestion for the recruitment of males and females into nontraditional educational programs, must be consistently in effect to be successful. It is extremely important for each sex to feel it has been spoken to directly. Subtle intimations that <u>all</u> are welcome <u>will not</u> succeed in recruiting persons into nontraditional areas.

It has been found that women respond favorably to role models (e.g., a female who is a student or a worker in a nontraditional program). They also are often influenced by male teachers in nontraditional programs if those teachers give them support and encouragement. Both males and females respond when they see pictures of persons of the same sex as themselves performing tasks considered nontraditional.

Students report that they do not want to find new obstacles to overcome when they have half-finished a program. Likewise, students do not want to be reassured about the importance of work satisfaction only to discover that the low pay was de-emphasized or not mentioned.

As might be expected, males and females do not wish to be recruited to be token members of any occupation or to meet quotas. Most research indicates that those students enrolled in nontraditional programs are more likely to succeed if they are provided with a support group or support activities periodically during the program period. There are six common guidelines among most of the strategies used in reaching female and male students.

1. Invite role models to speak to prospective students or to take part in panel discussions.

2. Be sure that bulletin-board displays or posters displayed in school halls are not located where they will only be seen by persons already interested in the program; select neutral locations.

3. Do not recruit students from sex-segregated classes. Recruit from general assemblies or general-education classes (English, math, etc.).

4. Provide male contact persons for male prospective students, and female contact persons for female prospective students. If this is not possible, be sure that the contact person is not going to discourage a person from entering a nontraditional program.

5. Discourage the labeling of students in formerly sex-segregated programs as "the boys" or "the girls" or "my boys" or "my girls."

6. Be sure that all of the materials developed indicate by picture or the written word that both males and females can study and work successfully in that program area--that success depends on interest and ability, not sex.

Sample Recruitment Strategies

What: Article or column for school newspaper

When: Periodically

Where: High school, community college, or university

Who: Students, teachers, or recruitment staff

How: Provide articles and advertisements for school newspapers that explain programs and tell about pioneering students. Encourage the school-newspaper staff to do a series of articles; try to include questionnaires on sex equity or sex stereotyping. Include people in pioneering jobs and those who have changed careers. Provide photographs to accompany articles. A regular column in the school newspaper would provide news about programs and about graduates of those programs.

What: Outside speakers

When: Anytime

Where: Classrooms, general assemblies, or where students will be exposed to the information

Who: Recruitment staff to secure volunteers from community

How: Arrange for females or males in nontraditional careers to prepare brief explanations of their jobs, their problems, and their rewards. Seek their willingness to become part of a support group for nontraditional students. Be sure contact names and numbers are available for interested students, not only contact persons in the school, but also people who could be contacted in the community at local business and industry sites.

What: Placement of recruitment posters in the community

When: Periodically

Where: Strategic locations to attract specific target groups

Who: Recruitment staff

How: To reach both males and females, locate posters in places where same-sex groups may congregate and spend some time (e.g., Girl Scout meeting places, YMCA or YWCA buildings, women's restrooms in public places or private businesses, [get permission], lunchrooms, shopping malls, beauty shops, doctors' and dentists' waiting rooms, supermarkets, exercise centers, home extention offices, laundromats). Picture males and females in nontraditional work situations. Show males and females of all ages, cultures, races, and physical conditions. Give wage-and-hour information in brief, and estimate schooltime for completion. Supply the name and telephone number of a contact person.

What: Radio and television spots (public service announcements)

When: Throughout the year

Where: Local radio or television station

Who: Recruitment staff or teachers

How: Use a female speaker and alternate culturally different voices with older female voices. Emphasize that education is for women, too, that particular programs are for women, and that particular institutions welcome women in all areas. Emphasize the personal satisfaction gained in an occupation that matches ones interests. Include examples of women choosing to combine work and family living.

What: Testimonial letters from successful graduates

When: Anytime

Where: School and community

Who: Teacher

How: From a follow-up study, contact graduates and help them prepare a letter that touches on present tasks, responsibilities, opportunities, helpful courses, salary range, and personal satisfaction. Place the letter and a current picture, if possible, on a centrally located bulletin board--not just the program-area bulletin board, otherwise only previously interested or enrolled students may see it. Consider publishing the letter in a school newspaper or program newsletter.

What: Display

When: Throughout the year

Where: Career-day locations, classrooms, neutral hallways, entrance areas

Who: Teachers, recruitment staff, students

How: Display people in nontraditional work situations by means of drawings or photographs. Present men and women of various ages, ethnic groups, and physical conditions. The critical factor is location. If a display is placed in the program classroom, only students already interested in or already enrolled in the program will learn of the opportunities. It is vital to reach uncommitted students with recruitment information. Encourage educators to exchange display space to inform students of other program areas.

Sample Recruitment/Retention Calendar

September	October	November	December
7 School starts 20 Visit by former students	9 Tour of Nontraditional work sites	18 Sex-Equity staff workshop	3 Display in Main Hall 1 week

January	February	March	April
25 Family night	5 Media spot releases	12 Letters to juniors	2 Poster contest 22 Fair (display)

Calendar Checklist

	Points	Yes	No
Activities scheduled through the year	2		
At least one activity for family awareness	3		
At least one activity to provide contact with nontraditional workers	4		
At least two activities to support students already in nontraditional programs	4		
At least one activity to interest younger students	2		
At least one activity in which peers do the recruitment	2		
Activities to involve key faculty in recruitment programs	2		
All media materials will be reviewed for gender fairness in content and location	3		
TOTAL	22		
TOTAL FOR MASTERY	20		

Unit Eight

Competency

Develop strategies to achieve schoolwide support for gender fairness.

Performance Objective

Given a group-generated list of examples of gender bias commonly found in schools, develop and describe at least three realistic strategies to achieve schoolwide support for gender fairness.

Learning Activities

Prerequisite: read "Sexism In Education," page 19.

Activity 1. Recall three or more incidents from your own high school experience in which you were discriminated against because of sex, or had firsthand knowledge of sex discrimination against someone else. (You may work in small groups.)

Activity 2. Generate a questionnaire for personal or telephone interviews of school staff members. See "Interview Guidelines," page 195.

Activity 3. Discuss the results of the interviews and generate a list of examples of gender bias.

Activity 4. Invite the "Title IX Coordinator" at your college or university to speak to the class.

Evaluation

Describe at least three realistic strategies for achieving schoolwide support for gender fairness. Strategies will include the following types of factors: the amount of time required, the estimated cost, and the level of key-personnel support that can be expected.

Interview Guidelines
Suggested Personal Interview Questions

Directions

Conduct a personal interview, either face-to-face or by telephone, of one or more school staff members (teachers, counselors, administrators, librarians, cooks, bus drivers, janitors, nurses, and school-board members). You may use any questions you wish, however, the following are suggested for inclusion:

1. What is your role (teacher, counselor, administrator, other) at this school?

2. How long have you been affiliated with this school?

3. Does this school provide equal pay for equal jobs?

4. Are girls and boys encouraged equally to take various course options? Are there any classes that are predominately made up of male or female students?

5. Do you feel that the policies and procedures of this school encourage the growth and well-being of each student, female or male?

6. Are textbooks reviewed for gender bias?

7. Are counselor tests and materials gender fair?

8. Are male and female sports budgets and facilities comparable?

9. Are there nontraditional role models on staff (e.g., female principal or administrator; male home-economics teacher)?

Unit Nine

Competency

Identify and develop strategies to counteract societal influences and cultural myths that hamper students.

Performance Objective

Given examples of societal and cultural sex-role stereotyping, develop at least two strategies to counteract gender influences on students.

Learning Activities

Prerequisite: read "Sexism In Education," page 19.

Activity 1. Examine a societal or cultural source that has traditionally promoted and reinforced sex-role stereotyping. (You may work in small groups.)
Source 1: Television Commercials
Source 2: Television Programs
Source 3: Magazines
Source 4: Personal Interviews
Work sheets for each source are on pages 197-201.

Activity 2. Report a summary of the findings to the class.

Activity 3. Examine the following issues in the class discussion:
1. How are male and female sex-role stereotypes in television, magazines, and personal interviews similar? Different?
2. What words and phrases would you use to describe the female- and male-role stereotypes you found?

3. What exceptions to the above stereotypes were noted?
4. How accurately do the stereotypes noted reflect the females and males you know?
5. Which do you think acts most powerfully in channeling people into conforming to sex-role stereotypes: (a) television, (b) magazines, (c) people you interact with on a daily basis? Why?
6. How can these influences be counteracted?

Evaluation

Describe at least two strategies in detail to counteract societal and cultural influences. Your descriptions may be in essay form.

Source: Television Commercials

Directions

Your television viewing for the next day will be not only relaxing, but also part of your homework. Watch as many television commercials as possible and fill out a chart like the one below for each commercial you analyze. If possible, try to analyze some commercials that sponsor shows for young children.

Commercial for:
Program:

Main Characters	Males	Females
Physical appearance		
Personality characteristics		
Activities in which the character is involved		

If there is a problem what is it? Who has the problem?

Who resolves the problem? How?

How does this commercial promote or inhibit sex-role stereotyping for men? For women?

Source: Television Programs

Directions

View as many television shows as possible and complete the following chart for each one. Be sure to analyze some shows that are viewed by young children.

Program:	Male	Female
Names of leading characters		
Personality characteristics		
Most frequent activities		
If there is a problem, what is it? Who has the problem?		
Who resolves the problem? How?		
How does this program promote or inhibit sex-role stereotyping for men? For women?		

Source: Magazines (Work Sheet)

Directions

For each advertisement in the magazine, answer the following questions.

Advertisements You Think Are Directed at Men

Male Female

Number of characters in advertisement

Activities of characters

Dress and physical appearance of characters

Products advertised

Advertisement's message (e.g., if you buy...)

Advertisements You Think Are Directed at Women

Male Female

Number of characters in advertisement

Activities of characters

Dress and physical appearance of characters

Products advertised

Advertisement's message (e.g., if you buy...)

Source: Magazines (Summary Sheet)

Name of magazine:

Intended audience:

Total number of advertisements:
Number directed at men:
Number directed at women:

List the activities illustrated in the advertisement.

Advertisements Directed at Men	Advertisements Directed at Women

Count the number of characters and the types of dress (e.g., casual, businesslike, formal, sportswear).

Advertisements Directed at Men	Advertisements Directed at Women

List the products advertised.

Advertisements Directed at Men	Advertisements Directed at Women

List the advertising messages.

Advertisements Directed at Men	Advertisements Directed at Women

Source: Personal Interviews

Directions

Choose several different people to interview. Try to interview both males and females, and people you do not know well in addition to friends and relatives. Explain that the interview will be anonymous and that it is for a class project. Then, complete the following interview form. Read each question; do not rephrase any of the questions. Each person will answer the question as well as he or she can.

1. Sex:
2. Age range:
   Under 10
   10-18
   19-30
   31-50
   Over 50
3. What is a "real man"?
4. What is a "real woman"?
5. What are some good jobs for women in our society?
6. What are some good jobs for men in our society?
7. In marriage should the man or the woman have the leadership role?
8. Would you vote for a woman to be president of the United States?

Unit Ten

Competency

Develop action plans to effect societal change outside the classroom.

Performance Objectives

Given a model action-plan format develop an action plan to promote gender fairness in society that can be implemented and evaluated.

Learning Activities

Prerequisite: complete Unit Nine

Activity 1. Read "Building Fairness to Effect Societal Change Outside the Classroom," page 203 and "The Influence of Parents on the Educational and Occupational Decision Making of Their Children," page 128.

Activity 2. Identify gender-fairness issues and problems that transcend the classroom. (You may work in small groups.)

Activity 3. Brainstorm ideas to be included in a building-fairness action plan to promote gender fairness in society. See "Brainstorming Instructions," page 204.

Activity 4. Develop a gender-fairness action plan to promote change. Use "Gender-Fairness Action Plan," page 204.

Activity 5. Evaluate gender-fairness action plans using the "Gender-Fairness Action Plan Evaluation Checklist" on page 205.

Evaluation

The completed action plan will be evaluated by students and course instructor using the checklist.

Building Fairness to Effect Societal Change Outside the Classroom

Building-fairness efforts, planned and implemented by teachers in their classrooms, go a long way toward improving access to vocational education programs for all students--regardless of gender. However, the efforts of teachers to build fairness may not transcend the classroom or the school building. Without positive reinforcement of fairness from parents, peers, employers, and co-workers, your efforts may be for naught. Thus, teachers, as professional educators, need to look beyond the classroom; they need to plan for and be involved with fairness activities in their communities.

You may question whether teachers have an impact on the values and stereotypes of society. Public education is a reflection of the community. If teachers can implement gender-fairness changes in their students, and if these changes spread into that community, then teachers will have begun to change community and societal values and perceptions. Of course, to be effective, teachers need to plan their actions. Poor planning may result in undesirable results.

There are several areas in which teachers can make a positive impact in expanding fairness ideas and concepts beyond the classroom. These include, but are not limited to, interactions with advisory-committee members, community organizations and agencies, parents and parent-teacher associations, professional education associations, local media and public-relations efforts. There are no pat solutions or simple answers, and each community has unique characteristics that must be analyzed and addressed.

Brainstorming Instructions

Key Question

What can be done to promote gender fairness in society?

1. Select a member of the group to serve as the leader.

2. Select a member of the group to serve as the recorder.

3. The group leader will head a short discussion to clarify the issues and problems to be addressed; focus on the key question.

4. The group leader will head a brainstorming session. During the brainstorming session all of the activities suggested are to be listed without comments about their merits. Attempt to list as many ideas as possible in rapid succession.

5. When the group has exhausted all ideas, make sure that each person receives a copy of the ideas recorded.

6. Individually evaluate and rank each activity listed in order of greatest potential for societal change and feasibility.

Gender-Fairness Action Plan

Directions

Follow these steps to develop a gender-fairness action plan to promote societal change.

1. Evaluate and rank the ideas and activities generated through brainstorming in order of greatest potential for societal change and feasibility.

2. Select one idea or activity from the top five ideas.

3. Identify the alternative ways this idea could be accomplished. Select one of the alternative ways and

list the steps that need to be accomplished to achieve it. Complete this planning-outline guide by providing the information requested.

4. Using the rating checklist, evaluate your fairness action plan.

Objective:

Step-by-step procedures:

Activity	Key Contacts	Schedule	Person Responsible	Date Accomplished

Comments:
Budget:
Resources needed:

Gender-Fairness Action-Plan Evaluation Checklist

	Yes	No
1. Is the language used in the plan gender-fair?		
2. Is the plan feasible?		

	Yes	No
3. Is the plan cost-effective?		
4. Is there adequate evidence that the plan has the potential to effect societal change?		
5. Can the plan be implemented within the existing time constraints?		
6. Are the activity steps sequenced in a logical order?		
7. Are the activities selected the most appropriate?		
8. Does the plan make efficient use of resources?		

For any items checked "No," provide a brief explanation or revise plan.

Unit Eleven

Competency

Conduct applied research to develop policies and programs to achieve gender fairness.

Performance Objective

Given a class-generated question or problem, design and conduct a research study and report the results in a research-article format.

Learning Activities

Prerequisite: read "Gender Bias in Schools," page 3, "Sexism in Education," page 19, "Confronting Sex Bias in Instruction Materials," page 98.

Activity 1. Locate, read, and report on three research studies relating to gender issues in schools.

Activity 2. Interview a researcher in sociology, psychology, political science, or another field about gender issues.

Activity 3. Identify a question or problem. (You may use a small-group or large-group discussion.) See suggested questions on page 208.

Activity 4. Design a research study, collect data, analyze the data, and report the findings in a research article.

Evaluation

Research article should follow established research-article guidelines. (Refer to APA manual, Turabian manual, specific journal guidelines; or your university's policy manual on publications.

Suggested Research Questions

1. To what degree do staff exhibit gender-fair behavior in the school?

2. Which, if any, of a school system's policies or procedures are gender biased?

3. When elementary pupils are asked what career interests them, what percentage would choose nontraditional gender occupations?

4. What are the community's values in terms of gender fairness?

5. How many television commercials during an evening are gender biased in intent, word, or visual effect?

Summary

School employees who do not deal with the problems of gender bias head-on generate a negative environment for students. School employees who allow students to be treated according to stereotypes about culturally appropriate roles and behaviors generate a negative environment for students.

To offset this negative environment for gender fairness, teachers must develop competencies in gender-fair teaching that will result in an improved environment for all students. The first step is to become aware of the effects of gender bias on members of society; the second step, identify personal biases and how those biases have affected the teacher. The most visible aspect of gender-fair teaching is the verbal and nonverbal interaction with male and female students in the classroom. Being able to spot unfairness is just the beginning; teachers wanting to offset the negative environment will need to practice gender-fair interactions until they become habitual. In addition, gender-fair teachers need to be able to recognize and choose gender-fair curriculum materials and counteract gender-biased materials. They must also be skilled at encouraging students to broaden their occupational choices beyond those they may have considered because they met cultural expectations. This competency is closely tied to the competency in recruiting students into nontraditional fields and providing the kinds of experiences and activities that will enable them to remain in these programs. Practicing gender-fair teachers will also find themselves actively seeking strategies to achieve schoolwide support for gender fairness. When gender fairness has been mastered and becomes a commonplace teacher philosophy, teachers will also seek strategies to counteract societal influences and cultural myths outside the classroom that hamper students choices.

The final rating sheet, "Gender-Fair Teaching Rating Sheet," can be used to provide information for improvement for a practicing teacher or for a pre-service teacher. It can serve as a periodic reminder of all the competencies that need to be in evidence in classrooms across the nation to guarantee all students' freedoms.

Gender-Fair-Teaching Rating Sheet

	Yes	No
1. I am aware of gender biases in schools and how they affect students.	___	___
2. I know my own gender biases and how they have affected my students and me.	___	___
3. In verbal interaction:		
a. I praise males and females equally for academic and nonacademic behaviors.	___	___
b. I critize males and females equally for intellectual quality and effort in academic concerns.	___	___
c. My criticism of males and females is equally harsh or mild in non-academic concerns.	___	___
d. I ask an equal number of low-level and high-level questions to females and males.	___	___

	Yes	No
4. In nonverbal interaction:		
a. I maintain eye contact with male and female students on an equal basis.	___	___
b. I position myself in the classroom with respect to students on an equal basis.	___	___
c. I use reinforcement behaviors equally.	___	___
d. I provide equal "wait time" to females and males.	___	___
e. I arrange gender-fair seating and group-work tasks.	___	___
f. I equally distribute assigned tasks.	___	___
5. I use only gender-fair curriculum materials.	___	___
6. I openly deal with gender-biased materials to counteract their effects on students.	___	___
7. I encourage nontraditional career options.	___	___
8. I provide nontraditional role models for my students.	___	___
9. I recruit students who are nontraditional for my class.	___	___

	Yes	No
10. I provide support for nontraditional students to remain in a non-traditional program.	___	___
11. I make suggestions for policies and procedures in my school that will improve schoolwide gender fairness.	___	___
12. I use strategies to counteract societal influences and cultural myths that hamper students.	___	___
13. I follow an action plan to promote gender fairness in society.	___	___
14. I read and use the results of applied research to improve gender fairness in my class.	___	___
15. I conduct research in my field on aspects of gender fairness and report my findings in journals where my peers can benefit from my studies.	___	___

TOTAL 15
Mastery Level 12